And Such Were Some of You!

One Man's Walk Out
Of the Gay lifestyle

By Anthony A. Falzarano

xulon PRESS

And Such Were Some of You!
One Man's Walk Out Of the Gay lifestyle
by Anthony A. Falzarano

Printed in the United States of America

ISBN 978-1-60647-386-3

Unless otherwise indicated, Bible quotations are taken from The New King James Version. Copyright © 2004 by Zondervan Press.

"Kate Kuhner Photography"

www.xulonpress.com

TABLE OF CONTENTS

I would like to dedicate this book to the glory of God the Father, Jesus Christ— His Son and to the Holy Spirit and to the brave courageous men and women who have taken the valiant step towards sexual wholeness.

I would also like to thank God for my very supportive wife of 25 years — Dianne, and for my lovely daughter Mary Victoria and my prized son Carter.

The Lord used many people that either greatly assisted me in my healing process or helped me to establish Parents & Friends Ministries. I would like to acknowledge them and have listed them below.

Dr. Elizabeth Moberly
Mr. & Mrs. Allen (Willa) Medinger/ Regeneration Ex-
    gay Ministries
Rev. Earle Fox
Sexaholics Anonymous
Mrs. Le Anne Payne/ Pastoral Care Ministries
Mr. Tyler Torgerson
Mr. Bob Davies/ former Executive Director of Exodus
    International
Mr. Pat Robertson/ The 700 Club
Mr. Gary Bauer/ The Family Research Council
Mr. Robert Knight/ The Family Research Council
Mr. Sy Rogers
Rev. & Mrs. Stuart McAlpine
Mr. Joe Dallas
Mr. Christopher Redder
Mr. Steve Comrie

Mr. Murray Nimmo
Miss Starla Allen
Mr. & Mrs. Tim (Janis) Dimond
Mr. & Mrs. Anthony Eller
Miss Elaine Sinnard & Miss Penny Dalton
Miss Mary Ada Malavolti
Mr. Dan Borchers

Do you not know that the unrighteous **will not** inherit the kingdom of God? Do not be **deceived,** neither fornicators, nor idolaters, nor adulterers, nor **homosexuals, nor sodomites,** nor thieves, nor covetous, nor drunkards, nor revilers, nor extortioners will inherit the kingdom of God. **And such were some of you, but you were washed, but you were sanctified, but you were justified** in the Name of the Lord Jesus Christ and by the Spirit of our God.

— — 1 Corinthians 6: 9-11, NKJV

CHAPTER 1

THE EARLY YEARS

The car pulled onto the circular drive of the stately Washington Club at Dupont Circle in Washington, DC that cold evening in February. The driver opened the door as my daughter and her escort stepped out of their car. Mary Victoria had been waiting for her *coming out* party for quite sometime. She was wearing the most stunning creamy white silk organza evening gown that any young debutante could dream of. In her perfectly coifed hair, she wore a beautiful tiara that sparkled in the evening light.

Her escort, a handsome young man from school, gently reached for her gloved hand. A wristlet of tiny pink tea roses that he had given to her earlier that evening graced her right arm. The couple seemed to be floating on air as the two of them whisked through the entrance of the club into the lavishly appointed entrance hall. After quickly dropping their outer coats they raced up the grand winding marble staircase that was the hallmark of the elegant Washington Club and were immediately greeted by the many guests that were invited to be a part of our daughter's special evening.

Mary Victoria was glowing as many of her friends hugged her and commented on how beautiful she looked. Any parents would have welcomed the opportunity to see their daughter enjoy such a beautiful event. The delight that was apparent in her demeanor that evening is one I will never forget.

After Mary Victoria and her mother welcomed most of the guests in the upstairs foyer, we all moved into the ballroom for a wonderful evening of dinner and dancing. After the toast and a prayer of thanks to God for Mary's life, I walked up to my daughter and asked her for the first dance of the evening. She graciously accepted as I led her to the dance floor. We had selected the *Waltz from the Nutcracker Suite* earlier that day and as the music began to play I placed my one hand in hers as I grabbed the small of her waist with my other. It was a classic scene, the beautiful debutante daughter radiant in her creamy white organza evening gown and the doting father in his dinner tails. My little "peanut" had grown-up. She wasn't just my little daughter any longer; she was now a young lady. Halfway through that first dance Matthew, her date, walked up from behind and tapped me on the shoulder and asked if he could interrupt? I politely agreed as I placed my daughter's hand in his and left the dance floor.

As I watched them from the edge of the dance floor a tear began to well up in my eyes. To witness the purity that emulated from both of them was memorable. This chapter of me and my wife's responsibility of raising our daughter in chastity and holiness was coming to an conclusion.

That evening was what a traditional *coming out* party was supposed to be. Something beautiful, something gay; a special dance usually hosted by the parents of a young lady as a means of introducing her to society as she comes of age.

Unfortunately, as I reflect on that wonderful night in my daughter's life, a different kind of "coming out" party comes to mind. One that I experienced as I approached my manhood. A dark, newly defined different kind of *coming out* experience that appeared on the American horizon towards the end of the last century. One that now included men in its roster of eligibility. A coming out experience that sadly replaced the beauty and purity of the former.

The "coming out" that I experienced wasn't one that a family would typically celebrate and is seldom welcomed by a young person's parents. This was not a *coming of age* of lightness, but one of darkness. One that every parent dreads his or her child will ever participate in. A *coming of age* that began in my life coincidently also at the time of my 16th birthday as I innocently shopped in the local downtown one Saturday afternoon in 1972.

As I pulled open the heavy glass doors of a local depart-ment store, I soon realized that a man was standing behind me. Being raised with manners, I knew that the right thing to do was to hold the door open for him; I did just that. At the time, I didn't realize this simple act of courtesy would change my life forever and soon introduce me to a lifestyle that would hold me in its' grip for many years.

This seemingly friendly man in his mid-thirties thanked me for my kindness and quickly engaged me in conversa-tion; asking me why I had come to the downtown. He then asked if I was alone and when I naively answered, "yes"; he then asked if he could join me as I shopped noting that he too; was by himself.

This was the early 1970's. It was a very innocent time in America's past, when people still trusted each other. I was a lonely teenager who had very few friends and actu-ally welcomed this man's invitation to accompany me on my shopping trip. I had no idea that this man was a homosexual who preyed on young boys. I hardly even knew what a homo-sexual was and never imagined what he was planning.

After shopping around for a while we left the department store and began to walk down the main street of the down-town. As we were passing by the old Loew's Movie Theatre

I looked up and noticed the marquee listed the new *Beatle's* film *Yellow Submarine*. I commented to my new *friend* that I would love to see that movie sometime. Realizing an opportunity he quickly offered to take me to the film as his guest.

I was considered to be one of the "nice boys" in Bloomfield in the early 70's; in an age when being *nice* had started to be considered a negative attribute by the quickly changing mores of society. My "good boy" image needed some *healthy tarnishing*. I thought by seeing the film that I could brag to my friends about seeing the latest "in" movie. I was never really interested in the hippy/rock type music that had begun to permeate culture back then, but the *Beatle's* music interested me and I didn't see any harm in seeing it.

Never in a million years did I realize that accepting this seemingly innocent invitation would have exposed me to the dark world of the homosexual subculture. Without realizing this man had any ulterior motives I gladly accepted. He purchased the tickets and as we were passing through the lobby of the theatre; we both agreed how much fun it would be to sit up in the large, dark, *empty* balcony.

It was there in the balcony of the theatre that he put his hand on my leg, seduced me and later performed oral sex on me. After he was finished he got up and told me that he was going downstairs to get some candy and asked me if I wanted some. I was almost speechless after what I just experienced but got up enough courage to answer "no thanks".

After he went downstairs, the realization of what I had just participated in hit me like a ton of bricks. I remember the sick feeling in my stomach as I thought, "How could he even think of eating after what he just did? Ambivalent feelings of guilt, shame, pleasure and violation began to manifest. I had to get out of there and quickly exited the movie theatre before he returned.

As I traveled back to the suburbs on the trolley car a million thoughts began to run through my head… I must be a homosexual too...what made him think that I would allow him to do such a thing? ...Why didn't I tell him to stop the minute he put his hand on my leg? And then the greatest guilt feeling of all was the fact that the act itself was somewhat pleasurable.

The nauseous feeling in the pit of my stomach returned as I began to obsess about the thought that maybe I had sent some kind of signal to this man that I was *available*. I hardly knew what it meant to be a homosexual; however the confusing feelings that were running through my head were tormenting me. Is it true?... I can't believe it.... No, it can't be!... My emotions were going back and forth and I was ill prepared to handle this.

As I arrived in my neighborhood I began to walk up the hill towards my house. I ran into my twin brother and his friends. I had mixed feelings of whether to tell them or not. They would often ridicule me because I was so *square* and they were so with it. In my warped false-masculine mindset, I thought if I told them that this gay guy performed oral sex on me, they would think that it was cool and accept me.

As with most boys who are sexually confused, I was trying desperately to fit in. They would smoke pot and I would tell them that it was wrong. They hardly tolerated school and I loved it. In hindsight, I now realize that God has his hand on me. The Lord was protecting me from the false masculine, but the immoral tide of evil that continued to move into America was redefining what was right and wrong. Teenagers in the mid -70's were now openly talking about pre-marital sex and commonly looking at pornography without much remorse.

Most of the parents didn't even realize what was going on and were allowing their children to attend rock concerts where a whole plethora of immorality encompassed them. There weren't enough voices in the *public arena* countering the *new waves of unholy liberalism* that seemed to be permeating our culture. Biblical morality was being drowned out by the "new morality"

The Church wasn't properly communicating the message that the behavior that the "straight boys" were participating in was as equally sinful in God's eyes as homosexuality was. Now that I am a Christian, I fully understand that *pseudo-macho* behavior is not anymore Godly than homosexual behavior. It's now so clear to me that my brother and his friends were in as much spiritual jeopardy as I was for living a homosexual lifestyle.

According to 1 Corinthians, 6; 9-10, it doesn't matter whether you are heterosexually promiscuous, alcoholic, homosexual, steal or cheat on your wife; if you don't repent of these sins in your lifetime you will **not** inherit heaven. God does not show favoritism!

As you would have probably guessed, when I did tell my brother and his friends about my sexual-encounter it wound up being a disaster. The minute I told them, I noticed my brother's eyes widen in horror as he exclaimed, "You did what? Are you crazy? That's disgusting!" This obviously did not help my popularity with the guys, in fact it further alienated them from me.

How did all of this happen to me? What events in my early childhood development lead me down this path? What early life experiences set the stage for my homosexual orientation? Why was I such a loner who needed male friendships so desperately? Why didn't I bond with the other boys in my peer group? Looking back on some of my early childhood experiences may shed some light on what led me down this path...

I was born in northern New Jersey to middle-class parents of Italian descent. At the time they had been married for over 20 years and already had five sons After deciding to try one more time to have a daughter they wound up having twin boys. I was one of the twins born that warm summer day in

July of 1956. My parents were both 40 years old at the time and now had seven boys ranging in age from newborn to 18 years old.

There wasn't a lot of money for extras, but by God's provision we had a nice comfortable home-life. Mom wore the "pants" in the house and took care of most of the finances. Because she was thrifty with a dollar, we always ate well and were well dressed. With dad's *middle-class* salary, it was amazing that they were able to pay off the mortgage on our house in 12 years and provide all the creature comforts that we needed.

Dad was a gifted tool and die maker. Unfortunately, he was not able to complete high school because he had to leave school to help support his family during the Depression. I remember him to be a brilliant craftsman, but I suspect that his employer probably took advantage of his lack of a formal education and didn't compensate him properly.

My mother had an inner strength that is rarely seen in the women of today. She truly enjoyed being a housewife. She certainly had her shortcomings, which I will refer to later; but when I reflect back on my upbringing, I am in awe of the sacrifices that she made for my father and their seven sons.

I have many fond memories of mornings in the Falzarano home. Mom would wake up every day at around 6 o'clock to make my father a full breakfast before he would take off for work. Then I knew that it was time for me to get up for school because I would often overhear Mom singing *Hello Again* along with radio personality *Herb Oscar Anderson* as his popular radio show of the 60's would come on in the morning. Each day she would prepare a full breakfast for all seven boys in between catching up on her daily clothes ironing which amounted to over 50 shirts a week. Preferring not to have a dishwasher or even a clothes dryer, she was definitely "old school". Mom enjoyed being a housewife and always seemed to be content with what dad was able to provide.

Mother rarely said "I love you" but she was the type who showed her love for her family in so many ways. Mother died a few years ago at the age of eighty-seven, but even up to the very end she still has 80% of the "steam-power" of her younger days. She's was rarely ill and rarely took medicine. Many people from my old hometown continue to give me testimony of what a blessing my mother has been to the old neighborhood.

She obviously was quite an influence on my life. And because I was so unhealthily attached to her, I picked up a lot of her good character traits and unfortunately, some of the bad ones.

My mom and dad were married for 50 years before he died of a heart attack in 1987. He immigrated to the United States in 1923 the third son of eight children of Italian-born parents. My father was a devoted husband to my mom. He was monogamous, rarely drank and hardly complained. However because of the physical demand of his job, his worries about finances and the demands of caring for a very large family, he rarely spent much time with me.

Although he was at home every night after work, he was the classic "psychologically absentee" father. We would all have dinner together as a family, but shortly thereafter he would retreat to the family room and soon fall asleep in his recliner watching television or listening to his Italian opera records.

He never taught me how to play sports because he never learned these skills from his own father and to make matters worse, they didn't play traditional American sports in Italy. This seriously impeded my assimilation into traditional American culture. None of the guys wanted to play bocce`. By the time I started elementary school I was already feeling inferior to the other boys.

Because my father worked so hard, my mom would be the one to take me to Cub Scout meetings and other functions. Her intentions were good however; this was embarrassing, because all the other boys were at Scouts with their fathers. We were raised in a nominal-Catholic Christian home. I couldn't quote scripture by memory, but learned about my faith through good example at home and at church. It was a pretty moral household where swearing wasn't even allowed. Just like every other Catholic kid in those days, I attended CCD, receiving my first Holy Communion and Confirmation, but because the "fresh-air" of renewal of Vatican II had just begun to blow through the Church, my faith in Jesus Christ was nominal. I knew Jesus as Savior but not as Lord of my life.

My father would march us all off to church on Sunday while my mother prepared the big Sunday afternoon meal. Every Sunday my dad would send the younger children to church, only rarely accompanying them there himself and participating in any of our other activities. Most of the time he would be resting or slipping-out to his Italian-American social club to play bocce. That was his escape from the pressures of his family and life in general.

Mom would send my twin brother and me to bed after "The Mickey Mouse Club." She exercised most of the discipline in the home. When she spoke, we listened, and if we didn't, out came the wooden spoon. (She went through dozens of them). My older brothers eventually discovered that they could take them out of her hand and break them. If we saw the wooden spoon come out, that meant we had better listen. Dad would usually be broughtn only to discipline us if Mom felt that we were totally out of control. My father was never abusive, I seldom remember him having to "use the belt" to discipline any of us. Overall he was a very kind man.

By the time my twin brother and I were old enough to come out of our cribs, my two eldest brothers, who were then in there twenties, were married. There were only three bedrooms in our house. The master bedroom was large and easily accommodated two double beds. Four of us slept in that room. Space wise, things were a bit tight at the house but at that time most people were having large families. Nobody thought of himself as deprived!

My father and mother never learned to drive a car. In the 50's and 60's people were able to function in their self-sufficient hamlets. We would take a bus or trolley car to downtown Newark, New Jersey for the more important shopping and would seldom have to go into New York. Shopping malls either didn't exist, or had not replaced the downtown. As my older brothers came of age, my parents would help them purchase their own cars. Under the circumstances I am amazed how well our family prospered in those days.

CHAPTER 2

HOW DID I END UP THIS WAY?

I began elementary school in 1962 and loved it. I was a precocious child, the "darling" of my first three teachers. I can remember my first-grade teacher taking a strong liking to me. She affirmed my intelligence in a healthy way. This was very good for my developing self-esteem. The elementary school that I attended thought I possessed a level of intelligence beyond my years and was even thinking of advancing me a grade, which my parents decided against.

Then as I entered the third-grade I was assigned to "the teacher from hell." Mrs. Collier was a very bitter person and didn't seem to care for the boys. She just thought I was too "big for my britches" and unfortunately decided that it was her job that year to cut me down to size. Within one year she was quite successful in destroying most of the healthy self-esteem that had begun to develop in my early years at school.

I was a pretty popular kid up until that time. But because she constantly would cut me down in front of the other kids, my popularity plummeted. I began to be ostracized by my peer group.

In fairness to her I do have to say that my personality at that time might have approached the level of arrogant; but this teacher's discipline towards me was outright abusive. Whenever someone in class did something wrong and she didn't know who did it, she would immediately accuse me in front of the rest of the class of being the instigator. I feared her wrath so much that after a while I began to admit that I was responsible for the wrongdoings because I would fear her interrogations more than her punishments. She unfortunately was quite instrumental in the downward spiral that my life began to take. In retrospect, I remember that year as being a significant period that the devil began to claim a stronghold on me. It was a devastating time in my life and one that took a long time to recover from.

Between the fourth and fifth grade I began to be emotionally attracted to a male 5th grade teacher at school. Mr. Barton was the all-American type and naturally athletic. He also served as the gym teacher and took a genuine interest in most of the boys. We all hero-worshipped him.

He would attempt to help the more awkward boys improve their athletic skills and did his best to assist me, but by then my athletic development was far behind the other boys. As the boys were getting older my sports deficit became more apparent. After being one of the boys that was constantly humiliated because he was chosen as the last person on the baseball team, I started to give-up in side and withdraw.

I also have come to realize that I began to be drawn to other boys who had either physically or psychologically absent fathers. Most of the male peer group that I was friendly was also needy for male attention. In psychological terms, they were experiencing same-sex deficits. By the time I was 12, I had even engaged in minor unhealthy sexual exploration with some of these boys.

The feminine in me was overly developed. I remember an incident in the sixth grade when I expressed to my mom a desire to dress-up as a girl for Halloween. I not only received encouragement from her and her girlfriends, they helped me apply make-up and my mother even let me wear her mink-stole as part of my costume. This kind of behavior should have obviously been discouraged. This was not a healthy choice of Halloween costumes for a boy who was showing early signs of gender-confusion.

I received minimal male bonding from my older brothers. I was the "smarter one" and because my twin brother and my next oldest brother were a bit envious of my intelligence, they took great joy in excluding me. I was often excluded from their "inner circle" and often ridiculed. Academic education was not properly praised in my family. Most of the praise and support I did receive in regards to my intelligence was from my seven *female* teachers in grammar school. Much of my male bonding involved learning the false masculine. I learned how to be "culturally macho," but not as a true man formed in the image of Jesus.

I was also pretty much on my own in regards to my religious training. A call to holiness would not have been very celebrated in my home. I remember sitting in a pew towards the rear of St. Francis Xavier Church one Sunday when I was about nine years old. The priest was praying with the congregation for vocations and while he was praying I vividly remember hearing an inner voice telling me that I would serve God someday. But I never felt comfortable discussing this with my parents or any family members. I don't think that a vocation would have been encouraged in my family. I think that they would have considered it a weakness.

It is also important to point out that there was also some inappropriate touching and rubbing that two of my older siblings initiated with me. One of those two brothers turned out to be a homosexual and the other turned out to be a promiscuous heterosexual who wound up committing suicide in his late 20s.

By the time I entered junior high school my low self-esteem was obvious. Because of my high-test scores, I was placed with the high achievers; however I didn't have the overall polish that most of the other intelligent kids had been exposed to. Naturally this made me feel even more inadequate. My mother began to notice my feelings of inadequacy and did her best to relieve some of the tension; however my father's awareness of it was minimal.

My father did not know how to handle me and decided to push me back toward my mother. This obviously was a mistake. I believe that the pressures of being an immigrant, coupled with his lack of formal education along with the mental and physical demands of his job overwhelmed him. I do wish that he had been more of a Christian role model and had participated more closely in my upbringing. I no longer harbor any ill feelings for him and can now say that I loved him. Forgiving him for his absence in the formative years of my life was instrumental to my healing process. "Forgiveness for rejection or perceived rejection by the same-sex parent is crucial to the healing of a homosexual orientation," says psychologist, *Dr. Elizabeth Moberly* in her incredible book *Homosexuality, A New Christian Ethic*.

My life began to improve in the upper grades although I had many acquaintances but few close friends. I felt very weak physically and learned how to use my quickly developing verbal skills to avoid being beat-up at school. Junior high school was pretty rough on me. I grew up in a very ethnic Italian town where toughness reigned. I remember saying something smart-alecky to one of the bullies, and he reacted by taking my head and cracking it against a tile wall, breaking one of my front teeth. When puberty began and all the other boys started to be attracted to the opposite sex, I began to be sexually attracted to the same sex. It bothered me that I was not sexually attracted to girls and dating them was, for the most part, disastrous. I was a good- looking young man. The girls were attracted to me and I would have no problem finding a date, however, I felt very little attraction towards them. It was very frustrating because I didn't choose to be this way. I couldn't understand what was going on inside of me.

I tried many things to help awaken my adolescent heterosexuality. I joined the soccer team but couldn't handle the rejection from the other guys when they noticed how insecure I was.

I even became manager of the high school basketball team thinking that just being around the other guys would help my masculinity flourish. And then one day one of the guys stole some money from one of the player's locker. For some reason the head coach called me into his office and accused me of taking it and kicked me off the team. I was devastated that he would even accuse me. I had looked up to him as a role model and interpreted this as another father figure rejecting me. After the basketball incident occurred, I remember vividly deciding to "just give up". I really didn't have enough energy or support to continue fighting...I just began to close up inside.

When I look back on my childhood I sometimes think that the devil had placed a "KICK ME" sign on my back. I thank God that Jesus is the lifter of our heads. Satan wanted to destroy my life. One time my mother took me to a concert at church and a man followed me into the bathroom and tried to molest me. As he started to touch me, I knew instinctively this was wrong. I remember feeling so desperately needy inside. Part of me was crying out to be touched, however, the Holy Spirit's prompting told me to flee from the bathroom and I'm glad that I did.

That was the same year that I was molested by a pederast at the downtown movie theatre and then to add insult to injury, soon thereafter I was seduced by a teacher from another school at a National Key Club Convention in the Poconos.

The downward spiral into homosexuality intensified. I was a broken image of a young man; my psychosexual maturation had been arrested. My spiritual and psychological silhouette resembled a piece of Swiss cheese!

The spiritual attack directed towards me was intense. The undertow that was grabbing at me was overwhelming; I was being washed out to sea in a tide of immorality. Before becoming a Christian, I didn't even know what spiritual warfare was. **And when you're just a nominal Christian, coming against the devil is like fighting an atomic war with a water pistol!** Homosexual fantasies intensified and I was quickly becoming an addict to masturbation, and soon afterward I was introduced to a gay lawyer who would give me money to lie in bed with him, while we viewed his extensive porno collection. Much of the pornography especially in the '70's was very crude and focused on young heterosexual men being seduced by homosexuals.

Many of the objects of fantasy were men in authority like policemen and firemen. It is so obvious to me now that the producers of the gay pornography were feeding on homosexuals who had deep father deficits and were searching for a strong man or hero types in their fantasies. I would look at these "perfect" male specimens in the porno magazines and then compare them to my self and guess what; my inferiority complexes would be intensified...not lessened. **That's why pornography is like poison to a homosexual.**

Most homosexuals are envy addicts. Leanne Payne offers this example in her books *Crisis in Masculinity* and *The Broken Image* of "the cannibal instinct." A cannibal does not eat you necessarily because he is hungry. He eats you because he would like to have your spiritual attributes. She mentions that if a cannibal is chasing you, just act crazy and he won't touch you because he thinks that if he eats you that he will become crazy also. **Envy is one of the root causes of homosexuality that must be addressed in**

therapy. A great majority of homosexuals that I knew from the time I spent in the gay lifestyle had deep inferiority and envy issues. What's really incredible is that many of these homosexuals were attractive but couldn't believe this about themselves. Deep down inside they don't feel handsome or pretty. Many times if the child is ignored typically by having a psychologically or physically absent same-sex parent the child will interpret this as a rejection. When a child feels rejected, he's going to feel un-loved and that's where low self-esteem begins to gain a stronghold in a child's life. A parent *must* affirm his or her children's appearance and sexuality. If these characteristics are not reinforced or appreciated, the child will develop low self-esteem or an inferiority complex that will transfer to one's adult life until some kind of therapy is offered. All of this is detailed in *Dr. Elizabeth Moberly's* book, *Homosexuality: A New Christian Ethic*. She has remarkable insights into the root causes of homosexuality and is considered a pioneer in the area of sexual healing.

CHAPTER 3

THE "COMING OUT" PERIOD

⟨≈⟩

I had come out of the closet by my senior year of high school. It was 1973; the sexual revolution was peaking. I really felt like an anomaly because I was beginning to live a covert wild gay lifestyle; however I was still a virgin heterosexually. I longed to regain my purity. I wanted to be like the students whom I knew at school that were living chaste lives but at the same time I also envied the male students who were heterosexually active. One of the root deficits of one who struggles with homosexuality is envy. A homosexual male does not necessarily feel like a female... he feels *neutered*. He feels as if he doesn't measure up to the other guys and having sex with men only further intensifies one's inadequacies as a male. You're led to believe that by having sex with another man that you will become more whole and complete when in the reality the exact opposite occurs.

The man that molested me at the movie theatre that day mentioned to me afterwards that if I ever wanted to do *this* again; that I could meet other guys like him at a "gay bar" on Mulberry Street in downtown Newark. At first, when he mentioned this, I was appalled, and thought to myself "I would never do something like that again". **But a few months later; like a vampire needing a fresh supply of**

blood, I found myself being drawn to this gay bar which was located in downtown Newark, New Jersey.

It was a small hovel, on a dark street off the beaten path. Opening the door of that gay bar was the equivalent of opening Pandora's box. It led me into a lifestyle that held me captive for the next nine years of my life. The devil knew exactly what it would take to draw me into the gay scene. I clearly remember walking in and being noticed by all the men sitting around the very large bar. Unbeknownst to me, this was known as a "chicken bar." A chicken bar for the layman is a bar that traditionally attracts older homosexuals who seek out young men. The forty or fifty men that were there that night stared intently at me as I approached the bartender and ordered a beer. Nobody "carded" me – I was the type of person that any gay chicken bar owner would die to have step into his bar. I was good for business. Most gay bars back then were pretty seedy looking. This one was not. What was different about this bar is that it attracted a heterosexual daytime lunch crowd, but at night when the downtown closed down, the clientele changed significantly.

In a strange and demonic way, all of my insecurities drifted away as I looked at my reflection in the dimly lit mirrored walls. Literally for the first time in my life I felt beautiful. Within minutes these men began to walk up to me, asking my name and if they could buy me a drink.

The evil one knows how to work on a person's insecurities. If the devil showed me his "horns" that first night at that gay bar, I'm sure I would have never gone back again. However, he fed my wounded ego with doting father figures tripping all over themselves to pay attention to me. I was a goner!

I met a guy that night named Cliff. He was in his early thirties, attractive, educated and rich. After an hour of conversation he asked me if I would like to go home with him, and I accepted.

As our relationship developed, Cliff began to introduce me to *other* gays in the area and eventually to the wild gay subculture of 1970's New York City. He took me to two notorious gay bars on Christopher Street. One was called *Peter Rabbit* and the other *Ty's*. One must realize that this was 1973; it shocked me to see men dancing with men.

The New York gay scene was quite blatant. What was going on the City, and especially Greenwich Village, really did not move out into mainline gay America until the early 80's. The level of decadence was unimaginable! There were homosexual establishments called "back room" bars where public sex would take place. Hundreds of gay males in one room participated in orgies. There were literally over 150 gay establishments in New York City, in the 1970s, in the pre-AIDS days where all kinds of sexual appetites could be satisfied.

I started out seeking mainly monogamous relationships, but soon realized that it was not the norm for the New York gay subculture. The episode that gave me a glimpse of what was "up the road" for me in this lifestyle was the time I met an attractive schoolteacher named Richard at a bar one night in the City. He was in his late 20's, attractive and supposedly *unaffected* by the promiscuity of the gay lifestyle. After a brief conversation, he asked me if I wanted to go home with him. I agreed. After a quick drink at his nearby apartment, we became intimately involved. Afterwards, I turned over and was starting to drift off to sleep. Richard woke me up and mentioned that it probably wasn't a good idea for me to stay overnight because he was a schoolteacher and had to get up early in the morning. In a trusting manner, I agreed with him, quickly dressed, grabbed his phone number and agreed we would get together that coming weekend. I left his apartment and started walking back to the bar to retrieve my car in order to head back to Jersey. As I was sitting in my car, waiting for it to warm-up, I couldn't believe my eyes as I witnessed the new love of my life heading back to the bar to pick up another "trick". I felt cheap. Being naïve and only eighteen years old, I couldn't believe that the man with whom I had just had relations could be so insensitive and callous. In my eyes this man was wonderful and was a potential for a long-term romance. In his eyes I was a "trick," something to pass a few hours of a dull weeknight.

I was trying to impose my outdated middle-class value system of monogamy onto the loose value system of the gay world, which was futile. I soon began to get the message that I was "old fashioned" and would just have to get with it! Before long, I also became just as callous as Richard. I rapidly slipped down the slope into being a part of the promiscuous gay sub-culture. The current had become too strong. I was pushed out to sea. I had become sexually hooked. I couldn't control my behavior, *it was now controlling me.*

I had become a sexual addict even before I knew what that meant. For the typical homosexual who is dealing with low self-esteem, the indiscriminate gay world fills a large void; replacing true intimacy with sex. The *rush* of promiscuous sex was intoxicating. It became my drug of choice!

The Roy Cohn Years

One Sunday afternoon another life changing event occurred. I was walking down Christopher Street, which was the most popular gay hangout in *Greenwich Village*. I was heading toward the waterfront, which was a gay "pick-up" area dressed in a t-shirt and jeans. An attractive man in his early 30's drove by in his car and began to stare at me. He pulled his car over to the curb, approached me and introduced himself as Russell.

He asked me if I would like to join him for a dinner with some friends on the Upper East Side that night. I was very attracted to him, and wanted to go but told him that I would have to head back to New Jersey to change clothes. He gave me *the once over* and then said that I shouldn't worry about how I was dressed. I agreed to go, hopped into his car and we drove uptown to East 68th Street, near Madison Avenue, and after parking entered what I thought was the lobby of a very stylish building. After stepping inside the large entrance hall, Russell told me that this was his friend's home and asked me if I wanted to go up to one of the bedrooms to have sex before the party, and that's what we did.

We entered a vast, well-appointed bedroom that featured a large king-sized four-poster bed where the underside of the canopy was mirrored. What was also so peculiar about this room were the hundreds of frogs that were strategically placed all around it. It was late afternoon, the room was dark but I could still distinguish the basic floor plan of the room. As Russell and I lay down on the bed, I noticed that a man in his early forties was sleeping in the far corner of it. I whispered to Russell, "Who is that?" He replied, "Don't worry about him." I thought it quite odd that he was there, but my attraction for Russell soon distracted the queerness of the situation. Russell and I became intimate and soon thereafter, this sleeping man joined us for a menage-a-trois.

Afterwards when the lights came on, this older guy seemingly in his late 40's, introduced himself to me as Roy. He asked me if I would care to join a group of his friends for dinner at Tavern on the Green in Central Park. I mentioned that Russell had already mentioned the dinner and that I would like to accept his invitation but pointed out that I had not brought a change of clothes. He took a quick glance at my physique and directed me toward his dressing room. He the said, "It appears that you are about the same size as I am" and instructed me to pick out whatever I would like to wear.

I walked into this enormous dressing room with 50 or 60 suits running down one side on it, dozens of pairs of shoes, sweaters and silk ties in every imaginable color and style. This man's dressing room was almost the size of my bedroom. For an impressionable teenager from the suburbs this was something that one would only see in a movie. I was stunned! I couldn't believe that this was happening. It felt like a dream. Two hours ago I was walking down Christopher Street in a pair of blue jeans and a T-shirt and now here I am in this huge mansion in the most fashionable part of town in some stranger's dressing room. What was even more incredible was everything that I tried on fit me perfectly (even his shoes).

The man who owned this impressively, exquisite house on East 68th Street was Roy C. Cohn the young brash attorney who defended Senator McCarthy during the Communist trials of the late 1950's. He also represented the Schubert and Netherlander theatre families and some of the most notorious Mafia families. He was also legal counsel for the new, very popular discotheque, Studio 54. Studio, the multi-million dollar "disco of the elite" was the most talked about nightclub of the era.

After I dressed, Russell, Roy and I walked outside to the front of the house, where an elegant, antique chauffeur-driven Rolls Royce was waiting to whisk us off to the restaurant. I literally remember pinching myself in the car on the way to the restaurant thinking this was a dream. It was as if I were starring in the male version of Cinderella. It was just too incredible to believe.

As our car drove up in front of Tavern on the Green in the midst of Central Park, the doorman at the restaurant opened the car door with a deferential greeting, "Good evening, Mr. Cohn." Being 19 years old at the time I still wasn't able to distinguish who this man was. I didn't make the connection that he was *the Roy Cohn* of the McCarthy era.

Roy was very kind and generous towards Russell and me. Soon after our first course, an attractive young man walked up to our table and joined us. I quickly put two and two together and realized that this was Roy's date for the night. I didn't know what this guy was privy to, but I instinctively knew that if he asked me what I had done earlier in the day; that I shouldn't volunteer many details. It put me in a very precarious position. After dinner, Russell and I spent the night in a guest apartment located within the house, and, like the classic Cinderella story, the next morning I was back in my blue jeans and tee shirt. However unlike the Cinderella story, here I was that morning sitting in Roy's beautiful dining room being asked by the cook what I would care to have for breakfast. I could only imagine what she must have been thinking as she served these four gay guys breakfast. I also remember Roy (knowing that I was star-struck) pointing to the rear window of his dining room and saying, "Barbara Walters lives in the house behind me. We wave to each other quite often. She covers for me at black-tie social events so the public doesn't suspect that I'm gay."

What I soon began to realize as I began to put this whole puzzle together at breakfast, was that Russell was Roy's procurer. The meeting between Russell and me had been staged. Roy knew, because of his reputation, that he could not be seen cruising the streets of Greenwich Village picking up young men. Russell knew Roy's physical type and would attract them "into the web" via Russell's good looks. Once the two of them believed that they could trust the person they had brought to the house, Russell would then pass *the baton* to Roy.

Roy had a brilliant mind. He recalled that I had mentioned at dinner the night before my fondness for the theatre so after breakfast he asked me if I would care to see a Broadway show that night. Not realizing his law firm represented some of the finest theatre families in New York, I naively asked him, "What can you get tickets for? "And with a grin he remarked, "Name it!"

This was a dream come true. We went to dinner and the theatre that night, and it was the beginning of a relationship that continued for the next 2 ½ years.

I began to research more deeply into Roy's background and soon learned of his notorious reputation. I know that many people disliked him; however, I seldom witnessed the dark side of Roy because he was always very courteous to me. A kindness, which very few people ever realized he possessed. Exclusive of the sexual favors that he expected in return, everything that he offered me was extraordinary. He treated me like the son he never had. If you're going to be a "kept boy", one could not have been any more fortunate then to catch the eye of the infamous Roy C. Cohn.

Roy knew I needed additional social polish if we were going to be seen together in public. He was constantly instructing me on how to respond to different social situations. We wined and dined at the very best restaurants that New York could offer and attended the best shows that Broadway produced.

Roy was very paternal towards me. I'm convinced that he had my best interests at heart. One example of his concern for me was evident when I shared with him my frustration concerning a persistent acne problem that I suffered with. I had been seeing local dermatologists in the New Jersey suburbs that weren't very successful in clearing up the problem. He knew that this condition upset me terribly, so he sent me to the best naturopath on Park Avenue who cured my condition in a few months.

The Studio 54 Years

There were unforgettable fantasy evenings of being chauffeured around New York City in the Bentley, Rolls or Jaguar, going to premiere restaurants, and then ending up at Studio 54. When one of Roy's "gilded motor-carriages" would stroll up in front of Studio 54, it resembled the parting of the Red Sea. The bouncers would clear the crowd away from the car as they hastily pulled back the velvet rope to allow Roy and me entrance to the stately foyer of the world's most chic discotheque. I really couldn't believe that this was happening to me. Studio 54 was extremely popular. People would be willing to give their eyeteeth to be admitted to this exclusive club where anything went (most of which was illegal). There were no rules as we danced night after night into the wee hours of the morning alongside such well-known celebrities as Jackie Kennedy, Andy Warhol, Liza Minnelli, Halston, Christopher Reeves, Calvin Klein and even Frank Purdue (yes, the chicken man). One can only imagine how intoxicating this must have been for a young man from New Jersey. Just about anyone who was wealthy and notable, graced the halls of Studio 54 at least once.

Studio as it was fondly called, was the ultimate "power source" but I didn't realize at the time just how evil the source was. The devil is envious of God's omnipotent power. He can't duplicate it- but he can offer a close counterfeit.

The patrons that graced Studio's gilded doors were a surprising mix. There were the very beautiful, the famous, the rich, and, of course, the gay people, who were always granted access. And then for "the whipped cream on the cake," the *very odd* were invited to join the party- and the more odd the better.

Each night the owners wanted to create a very high-styled, whimsical floorshow utilizing the patrons as part of the overall merriment. Although the decoration, entertainment, embellishments, music and lighting were beyond most people's imaginations, the real attraction was the patrons that would show up. One night it would be Calvin Klein's newest model, another night it might be a gospel choir. One never knew what to expect. A group of us might show up one night for one of the "special parties" and notice that they spent $25,000 just on flowers and decorations. It was the grossest display of material wealth that one could imagine especially that it was in an area of New York City (Hell's Kitchen) where just a block away poverty flourished.

On the first level was the bar that had the infamous light show and dance floor. Roy was able to pull strings and I was given clearance to go into the complex music and lighting control booth, pushing dozens upon dozens of switches that operated the million dollar special effects lighting system. While I entertained myself with this diversion, Roy would disappear for a while into the famous *lower room*. There the club's owners would offer the top celebrities pure coke and assorted pills. Roy believed that this room was too much for me to handle and would never allow me to come down there with him. I thank God that I never entered that room.

While the "drug stuff" was going on in the downstairs room, the upper balcony was a hotbed for any kind of sexual activity that one might be interested in. Studio 54 was a hotbed of decadence in the late 70's: gay sex, threesomes, and orgies, whatever the carnal mind could imagine. I can only imagine how much venereal disease, HIV, and other diseases were transmitted in the infamous upper balcony of Studio. What was really peculiar was that the NYC police were fully aware of what was going on inside the club, however no one ever bothered us because the police were being *paid off.*

Many of the famous staff, owners and clientele are dead, Steve Rubell, Roy Cohn, Andy Wharhol are all gone. Ian Schrager is the only one that I know of that is still alive. A countless number of the physically beautiful waiters and patrons are dead.

The government finally closed the place down, not because of all the highly illegal activity that took place there, but because the IRS found out that the owners of the club were skimming millions of dollars off the top of their profits and pocketing it.

The "rush" in that place was a phenomenon- the power of evil was alluring. In retrospect, I fully understand that the devil knew that God had an anointing on my life, and presented me an incredible *distraction* as a means to blind me from seeing my true destiny. I procured a passage on the grand way to hell... hook, line and sinker. This was the final straw – the insatiable desire to be considered "included" by the chic upper echelons of gay society swept me out to sea.

Roy Cohn would constantly astonish me with all kinds of incredible diversions such as the surprise party that he held in my honor on my 21st birthday. It was held on a beautiful yacht one summer evening in July while we cruised Long Island Sound. Afterwards we all went for a midnight swim at the charming country house that he rented in Greenwich, Connecticut.

Spending time with him was literally like witnessing history being made. I was there when he helped found People Magazine. On one occasion I sat in his dining room the morning Aristotle Onassis called to let him know that he had decided to divorce Jackie Kennedy and needed some preliminary legal advice. Shortly after these divorce plans were made, Aristotle Onassis dropped dead, so most of the public didn't even know that a divorce was planned. I don't even know if Jackie knew.

This incredible new lifestyle was so unlike the way that I was raised. The devil offered me a great contract. He knew exactly what it would take to divert me from the Lord, and for a while he was successful. Though I had every material desire satisfied, I still yearned to have a monogamous rela-tionship with someone closer to my age. All of the diver-sions Roy provided could not drown out my desire to really try to fall in love. So after 2 ½ years of not being able to take it anymore, I ended our relationship. I was honest with him and told him that I was not in love with him. He was quite a realist and knew it wouldn't last forever. He didn't give up easily though; the next day his former boyfriend called me from Florida and balled me out and said, "Are you crazy? You broke up with Roy Cohn! I *used* him for years and he bought me a Bentley and a restaurant in Coral Gables when I broke-up with him." Roy's former-boyfriend told me to go back to him and just use him. I informed him that Roy was too nice a guy to take advantage of any longer.

At this point in my life, I knew that most of the good moral attributes that I was raised with had dissipated, however. I knew I could no longer continue this relationship no matter what fringe benefits it offered. I know that he was hurt, but Roy was a survivor, I'm sure that he recovered quickly when the next impressionable handsome young man appeared on his doorstep waiting to be wined and dined by the infamous Roy C. Cohn.

Roy was an extremely busy man, but terribly lonely. In addition to our relationship," he would have sex sometimes two or three nights a week with the most handsome male callboys that money could buy. He would fly them in from all parts of the country for a night of romance, and then they would be gone by the morning.

I really can't tell you why the relationship lasted as long as it did other than Roy's fascination with my quintessential middle-class upbringing. Roy was in the spotlight all of his life. His father was a well-known New York Circuit Court judge. He was considered one of the top ten defense attorneys in the United States but it was the McCarthy Communist Trials that really made, and, at the same time, broke him.

He was always in the limelight, and he enjoyed that very much; however, I believe all he really wanted was to have had a *normal* happy life. I am convinced that I represented that to him. I was straight appearing and was a pretty average "Joe." Why he wanted to have a relationship with me, when he could have had his pick from a stable of much more attractive young men is beyond me. It was obvious to Roy that I benefited greatly from being in a relationship with someone as well known as he, however I do believe that he knew that I really did care for him as a person.

Even after we broke up, we remained friends. While swimming in the ocean one day off the coast of Cape Cod at a gay seaside resort called Provincetown, I noticed a rather large yacht docked off-shore. As I was floating in the water looking curiously to see who owned the boat someone yelled out from it, "Hey Anthony! Is that you?" Of course it was Roy *and Russell* on one of their wild weekend escapades. They sent out a small "launch" to pull me out of the water and I spent the afternoon catching-up with both of them. Roy invited me to one of his infamous dinner parties that he was hosting that evening at his local beach house and I thought for old time sake that it would be wonderful to be there so I accepted. Roy was quite determined. Many lawyers and judges feared him for his courtroom prowess. He was a smallish man; however, he was very intimidating in the courtroom. One time I decided to buy a penthouse apartment, in the 40's near Park Avenue on Murray Hill. My mortgage was approved and we were ready to close on it when at the eleventh hour the co-op board turned me down. I was discouraged and called Roy, seeking legal counsel. After I explained to him the situation, his response wasn't, "I might be able to help you," it was, "*Do you want the apartment or not?*" meaning, all I had to say was yes, and he would have arranged it. I later decided against buying it, but I know that Roy would have taken care of the details if I really had wanted it. He was one of the most extraordinary people I have ever met, a classic example of a brilliant mind gone to waste. He had a tremendous impact on my life, and I will never forget him. Roy was a fascinating person to know. I realized that many people disliked him, and some people outright hated him. Current events, though, seem to be showing that Cohn and McCarthy weren't so "Red over-reactionary" as most people thought. I do believe, however, that the anti-anti-communist movement pushed by many in the liberal media soon turned the public against both of them. This sent Roy over the edge. And I don't believe he ever recovered. I believe that he felt betrayed and continued to lash out at America and all it stood for until he died. We remained friends until he died of complications from the AIDS virus in 1986 at the age of 59.

I graduated from college shortly after breaking up with Roy. I had received a standard business administration degree. My degree surely was not going to keep me in the style to which I had become accustomed. After thinking about my options, I decided to place an ad in the Village Voice under the "male escort" section. I couldn't believe that I was doing this, but the lifestyle that I had come to know dictated my actions. I had become accustomed to the jaded, opulent lifestyle of discotheques and summers at the beach. I had become very much involved in the "chic" gay sub-culture of Provincetown, East Hampton, Palm Beach, and Fire Island. I was used to winters in Florida and the Caribbean; sometimes taking six to eight vacations a year. I obviously had become quite spoiled.

Working as a gym instructor gave my double life a veneer of legitimacy. I was now being "kept" by a rich doctor in Philadelphia, who answered my classified ad. He was only 30 years old, somewhat attractive, and extremely busy. He would come up from Philadelphia every two weeks, spend a weekend with me and then return home. In return for my "companionship," he supported the lifestyle that I had grown accustomed to, which freed me up to continue my search for my "dream lover." Life was perfect!

CHAPTER 4

THE WINDS BEGIN TO CHANGE

Even with all of this in place I still couldn't find any true happiness in the gay lifestyle. I couldn't put my finger on it at the time, but even with all the tempting opportunities that the evil one offered, something in my life was terribly missing. Shortly before I moved to New York City, two events occurred in my life that altered it and laid the foundation for God's call for me to leave the gay lifestyle behind. Both events were quite extraordinary and unusual. It just goes to show you that the Lord works in marvelous and mysterious ways, and that even if a situation starts out evil, He can use it for His glory.

The first event coincided with the visit that John Paul II, the newly consecrated Pope, made to the United States in 1979. I was about 23 at the time and living an extremely reprobate life of sexual sin with very little conviction or regret.

I called my best friend Mark one day to see if he wanted to venture into New York after I heard that the Pope was going to be in New York City at a youth rally. He thought it would be a fun thing to do so we decided that we should go. It's kind of interesting that we both had a desire to see the Pope because although we were both raised Catholic; we were living a pretty scandalous lifestyle.

Mark and I both knew we were sinners. We still respected God and the Church. Even though many gay persons have become quite militant against the Church, deep down inside both of us knew the type of life that we were living was wrong.

Not once would I think about coming up against God or the Church! I thank Him that I was able to maintain a healthy reverence and fear of Him and that I did not become totally reprobate.

We took the train into the City and were standing somewhere in a large crowd near 38th Street on 5th Avenue in the pouring rain as the Pope concluded a Madison Square Garden youth rally. Quite a few times I was tempted to leave (because of the weather), but something deep inside gave me the forbearance to wait for him even though we had heard from the parade-route police that he had been detained because the rally was running behind schedule.

So Mark and I waited patiently in the cold rain until we began to hear the roar of sirens coming from the motorcade and noticed the police cars beginning to clear the parade route. And then, surprisingly, just as the Pope was leaving Madison Square Garden, the rain stopped and the bright sun began to shine. It was the most peculiar occurrence. The sunshine changed the personality of the crowd in a moment.

Minutes later, John Paul II went whizzing by in his *pope mobile*, happily waving to the patient crowds. The motorcade was headed towards Wall Street where he was scheduled to give a speech. Afterwards I yelled to Mark, "Let's get on a subway heading down towards Wall Street and maybe we can get a better view of him before he enters the arena where he will be speaking."

We quickly grabbed a packed subway; and as we were speeding downtown, I said to my friend, "Mark, I don't know why, but I've just got to hear the Pope's speech." Right after uttering these words, a woman standing behind me on this jammed New York City subway car turned to me and said, "I overheard you just say that you have a desire to hear the Pope's speech. I just happen to have an extra ticket...would you like it?" I looked at Mark; he looked at me and said, "You take it, this means more to you than to me." I thanked the lady for her generosity, and minutes later there we were on Wall Street waiting outside a large fenced area where he was soon to address the crowd.

I looked at my ticket and noticed that I had assigned a great seat in the 12th row *on the aisle!* Had I been a dignitary, I couldn't have asked for a better seat. After agreeing on a place where Mark and I could later meet, I presented my ticket and walked into the amphitheater. I quickly sat down and noticed the motorcade had just arrived and was about to approach the stage. They had removed the bulletproof cover from the *pope mobile*, John Paul was leaning over the edge of the vehicle blessing and shaking hands at random in the crowd. As the *pope mobile* passed my seat he noticed me and our eyes locked. He reached out, stretched and grabbed my extended hand. He looked me straight in the eye as he held on to my hand; and although it was for only three seconds, it was as if time stood still. He looked deep into my eyes and straight into my soul.

This Pope was pretty charismatic. His face exuded the love of Jesus! I believe that the Holy Spirit revealed to him just how much of a sinner I was and how much I needed to be touched. I had rarely felt such strong emotions. Love began to pour into my heart. It was an enormous injection of love that began to fill the emptiness of my soul. It was intense. After he released my hand and moved on, I felt like the about-to-be stoned woman caught in adultery that had been forgiven her sins.

Please don't misunderstand, I am in no way am I trying to deify this man; however, the Lord used John Paul as his instrument in a marvelous way that day. I felt a great amount of the guilt and the shame related to the lifestyle that I had been living begin to lift from me. Spiritually speaking it was as if he and I had just completed an extensive conversation. I felt empathy coming from him. It was very liberating, and although I continued in the lifestyle a few more years, I somehow realized that my gay days were numbered!

My second life-changing event took place soon after. A man contacted me through the personal ad that I had placed in the Advocate, a gay newspaper. We spoke on the telephone briefly and agreed to meet at my apartment in New Jersey. We had a sexual encounter that night; and immediately afterwards this man sat up in bed and apologized to me for what we had just done. He informed me that he had just sinned and had caused me to sin. Next he asked my forgiveness, and then told me that God didn't want him to be gay and then he looked me in the eyes and said, "And Anthony, God doesn't want you to be gay either."

I couldn't believe that he was talking about God after what we had just done but he aroused my curiosity. I informed him that I, too, was raised in a Christian home and knew that homosexuality was wrong. He then exclaimed, "Do you know that the Bible says that practicing homosexuals will not go to heaven." I replied, "I know that the Church teaches that homosexuality is a sin but I never knew that it was in the bible. Where does it say that?" He said, "I have a Bible, would you like to see it for yourself?" I then replied in a surprised manner, "You brought a Bible here tonight?" He then told me that he had brought a Bible in his coat pocket that night and went to retrieve it. What the devil used for evil that night God used for His glory, and my new friend

Tyler opened up the Bible and turned to 1Corinthians 6:9-11, which says, "Don't be deceived, practicing homosexuals **will not** inherit the kingdom of God." But the Good News is that verse 11 goes on to say, "**And such were some of you once** but you've been cleansed by the blood of Jesus and by the power of the Holy Spirit."

After our clandestine rendezvous, Tyler and I quickly became platonic friends. He began to teach me about the Word of God. He helped me to understand very clearly that God did not approve of this lifestyle. His began to disciple me, but shortly thereafter he was transferred with his job outside of New York and I never heard from him again. God used this man to take me farther along on a spiritual journey of revealing Himself through the Holy Scriptures and began to give me a glimpse of what He had in mind for me.

If you belong to God, His word will not return to you void. From that point on, even though I moved into New York City to try to drown out the voice of the Holy Spirit. God began gently to open my eyes to the realities of the gay world. He allowed most of the adventures that I experienced in the midst of *gay* New York to be very unfulfilling. He also continued to woo me until years later when I couldn't stand the life of sin that I was living any longer and eventually began to answer His call on my life.

CHAPTER 5

GOD DRAWS ME CLOSER TO HIM

To live in New York City in the 1970s, pre-AIDS days, was "paradise" for any homosexual. I had a beautifully furnished, rent-controlled apartment on the Upper East Side, worked as a gym instructor near Sutton Place, spent weekends in the Hamptons, Ft Lauderdale and Fire Island. However, all of these creature comforts could not drown out God's voice calling me to holiness and to abandon the gay lifestyle.

One of the last episodes that came to pass shortly before I left New York City occurred in Greenwich Village at a gay dance bar called, of all things, *The Saint*. The bar came to life usually at midnight. It was the hottest bar in New York. It had replaced the quickly fading *Studio 54*. It was a very large discotheque boasting three levels. It was a former theater that had been gutted and reconfigured into a very sleek elegant nightclub. The sound system and light show was considered to be state-of-the-art. The top level, which had been the upper tier of the balcony, had been turned into an orgy room. Anyone bored with the merry-making that was taking place on the lower levels could go upstairs and participate in any kind of debauchery imaginable. It was *the* place to be seen if you were gay in New York.

After involving myself in some sexual activity on the balcony level I was feeling exasperated because the act that I had just participated in was so unfulfilling, I hung over the railing despondently looking down towards the strobe-lit silhouetted dance floor. I saw hundreds of gay men in blue jeans, most of them shirtless, gyrating their muscular bodies on the dance floor. Most of them were drinking alcohol, sucking on rags soaked with the popular drug of the day, sticking poppers up their noses, and participants in the most chic gay parties in town, yet at the same time, looking so miserably empty and desperate.

My soul began to cry for them and for me. The feeling of inner loneliness was excruciating. Just when I thought I couldn't take another minute of the pain, God spoke to me in the midst of all the activity. As I looked down onto the 1st level dance floor one hundred feet below He whispered ever so gently to me, "Anthony, this is what Hell is like," an insatiable perpetual orgy of darkness void of any of the joy of My presence.

I thought I was losing my mind. I thought God only spoke to Moses. I hardly even touched one drink. So if I were in my right mind, where could this voice have been coming from? I was beside myself. I wouldn't even have thought that God would even show up in such a dark place. His voice was haunting; I began to feel the conviction of the Holy Spirit. I was ashamed of where I was and what I had become. Who can relieve my agony? I had to leave this evil place and remember running out of the bar in disgust. It was early morning; the sun was beginning to come up. God had literally pulled back the "curtain of truth" and allowed me to see the gay sub-culture for what it really was: evil.

The bar was located in the midst of the meatpacking district. Real people were going to work, hard-working people. The stench and vulgarity of this rough neighborhood permeated my nostrils. I remember running through the streets trying to find a cab that would quickly transport me from this hellish place to my safe, pristine Upper East Side neighborhood, where everything was more ideal. I hailed a cab, rushed uptown, and ran up the stairs to my apartment. I quickly unlocked the door and dropped into bed, exhausted, and in tears wondering what was happening to me. I had so many layers of brokenness and sin that needed to be healed in my life, that if God had touched me with His love and healing hand all at once, I don't think I could have borne it.

I began to bargain with God. I obviously knew that being "kept" by this rich doctor was wrong and had to stop. I tried to convince myself that it wasn't prostitution, but I knew that it was. I had no idea that God would even be interested in redeeming my pitiable life after all the wicked things that I had done but He began to reveal Himself to me ever so gently. God was beginning to peel back the layers of sin in my life almost like an onion, one layer at a time.

There were three issues that I knew that I had to address immediately. The first was to end the relationship with Tom, the doctor. He was a wonderful man who took care of me and in his co-dependent love for me, tried to shield me from the world. However, I knew that it was time for the boy inside of me to grow up. It was time to earn a legitimate living, no matter how modest.

I'll never forget the weekend when I ended my *business* relationship with Tom. It was so scary to think that I would be giving up all these creature comforts. I made sure that I made it clear to Tom what a great friend he had been and not to take any of this personally. Then I told him that I didn't love him and what we were doing was wrong, that taking money from him for sex was insincere ... and because of that it had to end.

I also apologized for using him to support my selfish lifestyle. I told him that he was a good person and deserved better and I could no longer sleep with him. I then concluded by saying, "if he still wanted to be *my* friend, I wanted him to know that I wanted to be his.

As these words came out of my mouth, I remember hearing a voice scream at me, *"Are you crazy? Are you out of your mind, giving up tens of thousands of dollars with few strings attached, just because you're feeling a little guilty?"* I now know that that was a demonic voice trying to dissuade me.

The second thing I knew I had to do was to leave New York City. The gay spirit is very strong in many cities in America, however the demonic presence that covers the homosexual community in New York is especially powerful. God was calling me to leave this modern-day Sodom behind.

In retrospect, I now see God's divine plan to spare me from contacting AIDS. Right after I left New York City around 1980, the AIDS pandemic hit hard. In the early years the disease was spreading only in cities where there was a large promiscuous male homosexual population such as San Francisco, Los Angeles, Houston, New York and Miami. I lost many of my friends during the period of 1983-1993. AIDS was responsible for the death of over forty of them, most of whom were under the age of 42. Most of them were the most wonderful people you would ever want to meet, immensely gifted and talented yet in bondage to a sexual addiction that they never realized would be responsible for their demise. That's what's so disconcerting about the gay lifestyle: unbeknownst to them, the devil uses homosexuals as pawns to accomplish his tasks and then – because he is incapable of sincerity – allows them to contract disease and die!

I decided to move to Boston, the gay subculture there was quieter and more sedate. I could no longer afford to support myself legitimately in New York City. I knew I had to escape from the dark spiritual presence that dominated that area.

Not realizing that God was going to *heal* my homosexuality, I would try bargaining with Him. I would cry out ... I know the prostitution is wrong ... I know the promiscuity is equally wrong but surely You couldn't be upset if I maintained a monogamous relationship with another man? I really believed that God would bless such a relationship and that I would finally be at peace with the Lord.

God knew that I was hard-hearted. Everything that I asked Him for He allowed me to experience. Living in Boston, my fantasy was to meet a gay Harvard man, settle down, and "live happily ever after." Soon after moving there, a new friend of mine who owned the largest gay bar in Boston decided to have an all-college party. He invited gay people from all the major colleges in the greater Boston area to attend a dance. I decided to go to the party that night determined to meet a Harvard preppie. As I walked into the crowded bar that night, I soon realized it was filled with young college students who were being pulled into the gay lifestyle. Soon after I arrived, an attractive man walked up to me and asked me if I would like to dance. I agreed, and as we approached the dance floor, we exchanged names. While we were dancing, I asked him what college he was attending and he informed me that he was a student at Harvard University's Kennedy School of Government. He was bright, attractive, and witty – everything I could possibly desire in a boyfriend.

John and I began to date, quickly became seriously involved and then became boyfriends. I thought I had finally found true love. I even believed that God had brought us together. However, within six months I was climbing the walls, dying to get out of our relationship. John's "love" was choking me. I was incensed with myself. Here was the *perfect* relationship. Why couldn't I remain faithful to him?

John took our breakup pretty well. I cried the night when we broke up, not necessarily because of another failed relationship, but because of the reality that was becoming very apparent – that no man was ever going to satisfy me. The *gay revolution* was happening. Men who graduated from the Kennedy School of Government went on to become senators and congressmen. I jokingly thought I could be a future Senator's "spouse." I couldn't have *married* better – yet even this ideal relationship would not satisfy me.

My final gay relationship took place in Provincetown the summer of 1982. P-Town as it was called, was one of the first gay summer resorts. It was originally an artist's colony on Cape Cod. It attracted an artsy-crowd that included homosexuals. I was living in Boston at the time and would spend my summer weekends on the Cape. That particular summer I spent the entire season in Provincetown. It was that summer that I met Paul. He lived in Los Angeles and had just broken up with his boyfriend. His mother lived in suburban Boston. He would come up to visit her and then shoot out to the Cape for some carousing.

We met at a "tea dance" at the *Boat Slip*. He literally swept me off my feet. After his vacation ended he returned to Los Angeles and we began a dual-coastal relationship. This relationship overwhelmed me and I became dependent on him. I was even considering selling my home and business after the summer was over and moving to Los Angeles to be with him because I was in *love*. As I was coming to this decision and ready to share it with Paul, a letter arrived in the mail from him – it was a classic "Dear John". Paul informed me that he was going back to his old boyfriend and that our relationship was over. He didn't even have the courtesy to call me on the phone. I couldn't believe he would end the relationship via his word-processor. The break-up of this relationship really started to raise questions in my mind about the validity of the gay world. Questions such as…are gay people *really* happy and do gay relationships really last? God began to show me the painful truth about the gay lifestyle as I basked in the summer sun of *lovely* Provincetown.

Not realizing it at first, I became an unofficial observer of all the different lives and personalities that intermingled during a typical season at a gay resort. It resembled a live soap opera. There were a full-spectrum of "players" that showed up for the summer *performance* including a United States congressman and the mayor's brother, the drag queen who killed himself because he had been infected with the AIDS virus.

I observed the heavy drinking, drug use, public sex on the beach and the Mafia connections to the bars. Then came the enormous numbers of older gay men who were so lonely. Why didn't they have lovers?

There were prostitutes, transsexuals and transvestites all over the place. There was constant discord between the gay men and woman who couldn't get along with each other. Then came the public break-ups and altercations that gay and lesbian lovers would have when one of the partners would get caught cruising someone else. By the end of the summer I was beginning to realize that monogamous gay relationships were few and far between. I was quickly becoming disillusioned with the gay world.

All of what I experienced that summer was in God's plan for my life. After I returned to Boston that Fall of 1982 I was walking down the street near the Public Garden on my way to a porno bookstore to do something that I shouldn't have been doing. As I was crossing the street in front of the *Four Seasons Hotel* God spoke to me with a final warning and said, "Anthony, I have been patient with you long enough. You either leave the gay lifestyle behind now – or you will die of AIDS."

This was 1982. AIDS was just coming over the horizon. The gay community thought AIDS was something that was going to afflict a small number of unfortunate people, and that there would soon be a cure. No one knew that AIDS, which had its origins in the gay community, would soon become a pandemic and then spread into the heterosexual population. God was warning me in a prophetic way. He was literally telling me that this was my last chance. I knew in my heart that he really wanted me to leave the lifestyle entirely. Now He was making His message perfectly clear and was awaiting my response. I knew that I had to leave the gay lifestyle behind. I knew that I had to heed His call and deep down inside I knew this was my last chance. He had been patient with me long enough.

CHAPTER 6

THE BEGINNING
OF THE END

God chastises the ones that He loves and sometimes you think His presence in your life will kill you. However, He never gave me more than I could take. God had to allow me to come to the end of my rope so that I could learn the crucial lesson - that Jesus Christ is the only man who could ever satisfy the yearning within my soul.

I never understood, until I began to study the Bible, what idol worship really is. I never understood what Romans, Chapter 1, referred to when it spoke about "worshipping created beings rather than the Creator." I never thought of myself as an idolater. God showed me in a very clear way that I was hero-worshipping man, that this was idolatrous behavior. He began to show me that man would always let me down but that He would always be there to support me.

Scripture says "that Godly sorrow leads to repentance." I began to experience a depression but it wasn't a morbid sadness. *It wasn't that I wanted to kill myself or anything like that.* It was an introspective sorrow that didn't originate from an evil source, but from a holy one.

God really had me begin to take an inventory of myself. I began to realize that I had been living my entire adult life as a hedonistic, narcissistic self-absorbed homosexual. I began to compare my life with that of my twin brother who had just married the previous summer. The bitter truth that I would probably never marry, never enjoy the blessings of fatherhood by having children, and eventually leave no heirs, came to mind. This saddened me and I would sometimes weep but as I previously mentioned, the remorse that I was beginning to feel was comforting...it didn't feel bad! The Lord was chastising me because He loved me and wanted more for my life.

I went home during Christmas week to my parents. While I was home Dianne who was a friend of mine whom I had met through a gay friend five years earlier came by to visit. We knew each other when I lived in New York City. Dianne was heterosexual, yet enjoyed going out to the bars with her gay friends. She knew everything about my gay lifestyle and was never judgmental mainly because she too wasn't living the Christian life. She was leading a slightly promiscuous heterosexual lifestyle and was drinking heavily.

That Christmas Eve, Dianne and I attended a dinner party at my friend Louis' house. It was a lovely time; however, I just didn't feel comfortable being around my gay friends that night. I couldn't wait to leave the party so that Dianne and I could attend Christmas Eve midnight mass. It was the Cathedral of the Sacred Heart of Jesus in Newark, New Jersey. We walked into the large French Gothic structure shortly before midnight and for some reason, the crowded cathedral had only two seats to offer in the front pew. We quickly slipped in and began to participate in the beautiful Christmas Eve service.

During the course of the service God's voice again spoke to me and said, "Anthony, you are going to marry Dianne." Again, thinking that God only spoke to Moses, I looked over at Dianne in disbelief and I remember remarking to myself, "Where the heck did that come from, how strange?" What was really odd is that the voice continued to repeat this prophetic message the entire week that I was home visiting my parents. I remember returning to Boston thinking that I was losing my mind. The voice wouldn't cease till I was driven to take out a piece of stationery and write a note to Dianne which went something like this: *"Dear Dianne, you're gonna think this is really funny but a voice in church on Christmas Eve told me that I was going to marry you. Ha, ha, ha."...AAF.*

Feeling very foolish, I put the note into an envelope and mailed the letter immediately. I remember walking up to the mailbox and as I was dropping in the letter, saying to myself – "This is so ridiculous. Why am I doing this?" – while at the same time, beginning to realize that what I was doing was inspired. I returned to my apartment wanting to retrieve the letter from the mailbox but realizing that it was too late thinking when Dianne received the letter she would think that I was out of my mind.

A few days later a note from Dianne arrived in the mail. After the typical salutations, she began to explain that she too had heard a voice form God and then went on to say, "Anthony, you're gonna think this is really strange, **but in church on Christmas Eve a voice told me that I was going to marry you.**" She then went on to say, "I immediately discounted it because I thought you were happy being gay and had no desire to leave the gay lifestyle behind. The truth is, Anthony, I experienced a flood of romantic feelings for you at church that night but thought marriage was out of the question."

After reading the note, I quickly dialed her home in New Jersey. After I greeted her, I let her know that I had received her letter. We both began to laugh nervously. I then began to bare my soul to her and share that I had been quite content living as a homosexual for nine years up until recently. I told Dianne that I had anything a gay person could possibly want. In the natural realm, there should be no reason why I shouldn't be happy. I began to share how God was convicting me that the gay lifestyle was wrong. I recounted what God had spoken into my life the day that I was heading towards a porno bookstore. I told her that what I really wanted was to get married, have children, and a house with a white picket fence. I then told her all that I really ever wanted was a normal life.

"Anthony," Dianne then said, "I'm nearly 30 years old. I was raised in a Christian home. I have also fallen away from God. I have been heterosexually promiscuous. I am climbing the very empty, female corporate ladder at Citibank in New York. To handle all the pressures and long hours of my work, I have begun to drink heavily. I, too, am sick of my lifestyle. I, too, would like to get married and raise a family. I, too, would like to return to my Christian roots."

At that point I invited her to come up to Boston to talk about this more seriously. Dianne accepted my invitation, and within a few weeks, there we were, sitting in my condominium on Commonwealth Avenue, two sinners being called out of darkness, discussing the possibility of marrying and getting well together.

At the time, I had no idea that God was actually going to *heal* my homosexuality. I really didn't realize what He was planning. I thought the best that I could hope for was to leave my gay lifestyle behind and live as an abstinent homosexual married to a woman. Being weak in our faith and not realizing God's omnipotent power to heal damaged people, Dianne and I both agreed that if we were to marry, we would accept the limits of my dysfunction. Therefore, if I were "climbing the walls" in terms of my homosexual attractions, then it would be all right for me to have a one night stand once a year to defuse the pressure as long as

I was discreet. Another example of how lost we both were and how little Dianne and I understood about the sanctity of marriage is revealed in the fact that she hosted a bachelor party the week before the wedding that she planned with one of my gay friends at the local gay bar in Boston. Dianne and I were both co-dependents. In truth she should have never agreed to any potential infidelity in the marriage. We were so young in our relationship with the Lord and couldn't envision what God had in store for us therefore she acquiesced to my request.

Now that I had agreed to change much of my own behavior, I had some requests for changes in Dianne's life. I asked that she pare down her heavy "social drinking" and discontinue the birth-control pills she was taking. I considered both of these habits could jeopardize Dianne and our future family's health and although she had curtailed most of her drinking recently, she would have been susceptible to alcoholism if she continued in earlier patterns. She agreed to both of my requests.

Knowing we had been totally honest with each and had now *cleared the air*, we then agreed to get married. I remember feeling very excited about the prospects of our upcoming nuptials but on the other hand feeling utterly mortified.

Breaking the news to my gay friends that I was leaving the lifestyle behind and getting married wasn't easy. They were in shock. I informed them that I was more dumbfounded than they were. Many of my friends were not supportive, I was no longer the "life of the party," a sexual partner, or a co-enabler of *their* lifestyle. Going straight was very threatening to them because it also brought the decadence of their own lives into the limelight.

Shortly after we were engaged, I went to see a friend who was a jeweler on Beacon Hill and selected a beautiful diamond engagement ring for my future wife thinking afterwards "Is this really happening?"

Something was happening inside of me. I was beginning to mature; I was becoming the man that God always intended me to be. It was terribly exciting but at the same time obviously very scary. God was re-parenting me and was taking me through this arduous task step by step.

In early February 1983 as we sat parked in front of the Waldorf Astoria in New York City, with much anxiety and hope, I asked Dianne to be my wife. She formally accepted my proposal; we kissed and set a wedding date for the first Sunday in October. I really believed that I needed at least a six-month engagement period in order to work on some serious issues that needed to be addressed before the ceremony. I had an awful amount of habits that needed changing before October 2nd rolled around!

Right after our engagement was announced, the spiritual warfare that I didn't realize I was under intensified. The following week I jumped on a plane to go to Rio de Janeiro to attend "Carnival" This was to be my final "fling". I naively thought I could work this gay thing out of my system before the wedding.

I arrived in Rio and, just as you would suspect, the devil set in my path three of the most beautiful men that I had ever had relations with. Satan knew that he was losing me. I'm sure that he even realized that God was going to heal me and then use me to help others come out of the gay lifestyle, so he pulled out all the guns that week at "Carnival."

The overt lewdness that is tolerated as part of the "Carnival" week is scandalous. It was the equivalent of spending a week in Sodom and Gomorrah. The blatant homosexual and heterosexual immorality even shocked *my* jaded personality. There was promiscuous public sexual activity on display all over the city. I couldn't even believe that the

City of Rio de Janeiro tolerated this unbridled behavior. This was too much, even for me.

As if there weren't enough temptations in my life already, one of the three guys I met wanted to come back to America and be my boyfriend. I was in the midst of a spiritual fight and was seriously losing the battle. But remarkably, even though Satan was offering me temporal, earthly perfection, I knew the choice that I had made and I was going to stick to it. I soon realized leaving the lifestyle behind wasn't going to be as easy as I had thought it would be.

One young man that I had relations with took me back to his parents' apartment for sex while the entire family was sleeping in the next room. It didn't even bother the parents, we all had breakfast the next morning, but the thought, of how I defiled that home made me sick to my stomach. I would have never previously have thought of committing such a dishonorable act.

The gay lifestyle consistently wears down your value system. Eventually one will exhibit behaviors that formerly would have made one blush. God was really *putting my nose in it*. He was showing me how low I had sunk. I remember getting on the airplane to come back to the United States abhorred by my outlandish behavior. He was showing me the difference between lust and love. As you might suspect, the sexual immorality was much more under control after the Rio disaster.

After returning home Dianne and I announced our engagement to her parents. They were very happy for us, obviously not realizing the lifestyles Dianne and I were leaving behind. On the surface we looked like the All-American couple. We hid our secret lives of sin very well.

We then went to visit my parents to break the news to them. They were very happy to hear the news however, my Italian-Jewish mother had to throw in one of her comments and said "This is great, Dianne, but do you *really* want to marry *him*?" *(Sic)*

My family is in the wedding business in New Jersey, Dianne's family are socialites, and I was a former-homosexual with impeccable taste. You can only imagine how grand the wedding was! I remember meeting the organist at the Church so we could select the music for the marriage ceremony and his remarking to me, "Gee I've never met a *groom* before who was so interested in the selection of the wedding music."

It was an extraordinary wedding, with 220 of our closest friends, acquaintances and relatives present. Imagine how stressful it was making the seating arrangements for the reception, as we attempted to keep so and so away from so and so.

We were married at the Cathedral of the Sacred Heart of Jesus in Newark, NJ, the same church in which we had both heard from God that previous Christmas Eve. The organist began to play the grand processional, and as her father escorted Dianne down the aisle, I remember saying to myself, "How beautiful she is." "How beautiful this day is… I couldn't believe that this day in my life had finally come. Tears began to well in my eyes.

As Dianne and I approached the altar, I looked out over the large expanse of the church. I could feel God's presence in the midst of what we were about to do. Although we were not permitted to see the ending of this storybook tale, I just knew that everything was going to work out. God was doing a new thing and was revealing His plan for our lives, chapter by chapter. As the priest was asking Dianne, *"Do you take Anthony to be your lawfully wedded husband,"* the clouds in the overcast sky literally burst open with rain. The thunder was so loud at that point in the ceremony that the priest paused. The lightning was so bright that it lit up the cathedral's numerous, fifty-foot-high stained-glass windows. It was unforgettable! The Holy Spirit spoke to me at that point and told me **that I was being ripped out of the clutches of Satan forever and that Dianne and I were being sanctified through the sacrament of marriage in which He was placing us.** Even those who attended the wedding knew something extraordinary had taken place that day. Years later, I remember Dianne's aunt remarking to me at a family function, "Oh, Anthony dear, I'll never forget all the thunder and lightning that day at your wedding. It was so incredible."

The wedding reception was held at the Women's Club of Glen Ridge, NJ. Try to imagine the mélange of wedding guests that filled the reception hall: Dianne's socialite family, my ethnic Italian family, Dianne's straight friends and my gay friends. Can you picture my *ditzy* former bar-buddy walking up to me during the cocktail reception and blurting out, "Hey, Anthony! Did you see that beefy waiter over there?" I turned to him in a state of shock and whispered, *"Otto, are you crazy? This is my wedding!"*

My brother and his wife gave us as a wedding present a beautiful honeymoon trip to Rome, and Monte Carlo. The honeymoon night happened a day later because we were so exhausted from the festivities of the day but went off well. My honeymoon jitters were calmed. I knew I wasn't a raging heterosexual yet, however, this new experience was not as traumatic as I anticipated. While there were no great fireworks that first time, this new sexual relationship with my wife was pleasurable. I soon realized that Dianne enjoyed the hugging, holding and closeness as well as sexual relations. It was obviously very different from the years of unfulfilling homosexual relationships. Relations with the opposite sex in the way God intended it to be was much more fulfilling.

CHAPTER 7

AND THEN THE
HONEYMOON WAS OVER

W e arrived home from our European wedding trip to our newly purchased honeymoon bungalow, an old gardener's cottage on a large estate in a Boston suburb. The first few months of marriage were perfectly fine. However, the actuality of walking straight out of the gay lifestyle into a heterosexual marriage without any therapy or sufficient premarital counseling soon hit.

In the first year of marriage I was unfaithful to Dianne three times. Not bad considering I was a sexual addict …but not good… considering that I called myself a Christian. The third time I was unfaithful, the Holy Spirit warned me that day that **He didn't call me out of homosexuality to be an adulterer."**

Six months after we were married, Dianne became pregnant with our first child. We both decided that it would be best to leave Boston and return home to New Jersey. We thought it best if our children could be raised around both sets of grandparents. Right before the baby came we left Boston and moved to New Jersey and bought a large six-bedroom colonial home in Summit, NJ.

I hypothesized: By leaving my old, familiar Boston *hangouts* behind, my personal demons would not jump in the suitcase and follow me to New Jersey. I assumed that if I just walked away from the gay world, my homosexuality would disappear. Boy, was I wrong! Can you imagine the pressures of being a newly married ex-gay with a pregnant wife, renovating a large old six-bedroom house, starting a new job, and living within twenty minutes of your in-laws? On top of all that, as I was sitting in my study one day the phone rang and it was a call from my former boyfriend, Ned Burns. I answered the phone and he said, "Anthony, this is Ned calling from Boston." After a while, he said, "Listen, I need to tell you something. I am dying of AIDS and my doctor asked me to call all my former sexual partners to let them know that they should be tested for the virus."

I was in absolute shock! After I hung up the phone, the reality of what I had done for the last nine years of my life hit me like a ton of bricks. I knew God had forgiven me for whatever I had done, however, I now began to understand that there are consequences for our sin. As I sat in the silence of my study I literally felt a hand on my shoulder push me to my knees. I cried out to God, "I know what I have done for the last nine years was sinning against you, I deserve to die. *But please, not my wife, not our baby! Don't let them suffer for what I have done!*"

AIDS researchers were just beginning to report that the virus was transmitted through sexual contact. At the time, I didn't realize that if I was HIV positive, I could transmit the virus to my wife through sexual relations. My naivete could have had far reaching consequences. Now realizing this, I cried out to God and made covenant with Him and promised; if He would give me a negative AIDS test result that I would get some real help for my sexual addiction.

Back in the early 80's, it took two weeks to get an AIDS test result and by God's grace the test came back *negative.*

I made a vow to Him that day and I know conclusively if I ever broke it by touching another man that I would be lost.

I remember one situation, during a weakened period of my life, having an opportunity to have an anonymous sexual encounter with an attractive man that I had met in a gay movie house. The temptation to fall sexually with him was severe and as I reached out my hands to touch him, God, the Holy Spirit, spoke to me and said, "**Do you remember our agreement?**" It scared the hell out of me. My hands quickly recoiled and I ran from the theatre that afternoon.

God was not kidding. He wanted to do a great work in me and this was not a game! I had promised God that I would never be unfaithful to my wife again and He was expecting me to hold my end of the bargain. By His grace, I have kept our agreement and have remained faithful to Dianne for over 24 years.

Our first child, Mary Victoria, was born in January of 1985. She was born healthy and possessed everything you could possibly want in a little girl. She was an absolutely beautiful child. I'll never forget being in the operating room with Dianne as Mary was being delivered. It was the most peculiar feeling. *First there were two of us and then there are three of us*! I remember leaving the hospital that morning and crying out to the Lord, "God, how am I going to take care of these two people? I don't even know how to take care of myself." But somehow I knew that God was in control and that it would be okay. Its very frightening going from being a narcissistic, self-centered homosexual and then into marriage and then into fatherhood. However, God has never let me down. God used Mary Victoria as an instrument of healing in my life. I was so weak in those early days. I wasn't acting out with men physically; however in the early days I had a hard time keeping my eyes from "cruising". I made a vow to God that whenever little Mary Victoria and I would be out in public and I would notice an attractive man walking down the street, as long as I was with her I asked God for the strength to "look away" from the temptation in my life. I didn't want to defile her in any way and with God's help I was successful 99% of the time.

What really kept me in a state of guilt in the early years of marriage was thinking that I was the only one that brought issues to our marriage. **What I soon realized was that Dianne had not only brought baggage to our marriage, she brought steamer trunks!**

It was quite naïve of me to think that Dianne's issues would have also disappeared once we walked down the aisle. Being involved in her career for a decade, and being raised in a house where her mom wasn't exactly the best homemaker, it became very apparent to me that Dianne could not cook or maintain our home. On top of that, Dianne had a new baby to care for. The house was a huge old Georgian colonial and was just too much for her. We began to have arguments over the tidiness of the house and the typical issues that newly weds fight over. I also believe my repressed homo-sexual desires were beginning to exacerbate the situation. The sexual acting out before marriage was my way to release steam. Now that I had committed my body to the Lord and to my wife in the holiness of marriage, the demons began to taunt me. I was beginning to climb the walls so I convinced myself that masturbation, pornography and fantasy weren't *really* sin, and they became my new sexual outlets. It was not a pretty picture.

After two years of marriage, most of which was living hell for both of us, we decided that it was time to see a Christian marriage counselor. We should have attended premarital counseling and as a consequence of not attending, we lacked the necessary coping skills to effectively handle marital conflicts and situations.

Being typical dysfunctional Christians; we didn't want anyone in town to know that we were experiencing problems; therefore we called the church in the next town for help. They recommended a *Christian* psychiatrist who specialized in marriage counseling. After only three sessions he told us in his office one afternoon that we should have never been married. He was insistent that the marriage should be annulled, and to add insult to injury, suggested that we do it as soon as possible."

What was *really* alarming is that we hadn't even shared the *heavy stuff* with him yet. He didn't even know about my former homosexual lifestyle and Dianne's premarital promiscuity or her former drinking problem.

After he communicated his "prescription" for our marriage I stood up from my chair in the counselor's office as righteous indignation began to well up inside of me and cried out saying, "We came to *you* because we know that our marriage is in trouble." We also decided to see you because the local church told us that you are a "Christian" marriage counselor. We believe that what God has joined together, that no man should put asunder. And we are paying you $75/hour to send us into divorce court?" Dianne and I were quite upset at him and let him know it as we walked out of his office. We hadn't expected this. We thought after listening to all of the issues that were affecting our marriage, he would then offer some advice on how it could be improved.

As we approached the parking lot we looked at each other and then hugged. I said, "Dianne, Do you want to get divorced? She said, "No!" I then said, "I know that God has called us to marry each other and if He has called us to this marriage, then He must have a plan to make it work.

What the devil used for evil that day in an attempt to break up our marriage, God used for His glory. We were being challenged to keep our vows; *for better or for worse, in sickness and in health, for richer and for poorer, till death do us part.*" And even if it *killed* us we were going to try our best to make this marriage work. This certainly was one of the sickest, poorest, worst points in our marriage but I believed that God would move us beyond this *storm* if we just held on.

After this tragedy at the *Christian-counselor-from-hell's* office, a new peace came over our marriage. Dianne and I began to attend church more regularly. We began to realize that only God could repair the times that the locusts had eaten out of both of our lives. We began to seek Him much more seriously and sure enough, our marriage began to improve.

Approximately three-and-a-half years into our marriage I received a phone call from a former boyfriend from Boston. His name was Fred. Fred and I were involved in the same profession. We were both architectural restorers. He informed me that he had moved to Washington, D.C., and there was a great demand for our work there.

He knew that Dianne and I were struggling financially because an economic recession had hit hard in 1986 and demand for projects in my field had temporarily dried-up in the greater New York City area. Fred said that if I were willing to move to Washington, there would be great opportunities for local projects in our field. He informed me that Washington was basically recession-proof and that the real estate market was doing quite well. He then mentioned that urban Washington, especially the Logan Circle area, was going through a revival.

Thanking him for his kind offer, I informed him that I had no interest in moving to Washington, DC and preferred to move back to Boston. He then said, "Why don't you and Dianne come down to Washington for the weekend, and I'll entertain you. I'll give you an insiders briefing on what's going on down here and *if* at the end of the weekend, if you are not impressed with what you see and the opportunities that are offered, then I won't push it again."

What I really didn't realize, God was using my former boyfriend as a vehicle in order to entice me to move to

Washington where I would be able to find some specific help for my sexual addition that wasn't readily available to me in New Jersey.

Dianne and I accepted Fred's invitation, came down to Washington, and fell in love with the nation's capital. We listed the New Jersey house on the real-estate market and were able to sell it at a good price even though the market was relatively stale. We were able to buy a house in the historic district in downtown Washington and I was the able to find some suitable projects to restore that were in my our neighborhood. Life was good...Dianne and I were prospering.

However, with all of the pressures of moving to a new city, my homosexual disorientation began to flare up again. I began to be tempted to "act out" but never allowing it to be with another person. I continued to rationalize in my mind that indulging into pornography, fantasy, and masturbation was okay since I was not acting out with men. Then in one day my life changed forever. As I was looking at the porno section in the back of the Washington *City Paper*, titillating myself with its content, my eye noticed a tiny quarter-inch ad. It simply read, "Are you a sexual addict? Do you want help? Sexaholics Anonymous (S.A.) group meets at St. Matthew's Cathedral in downtown Washington on Tuesday nights." In the sea of sexual pornographic sludge God directed my eye to that small ad that would begin my exodus from a homosexual neurosis.

CHAPTER 8

THE LIGHT AT THE END OF THE TUNNEL

That night I rushed down the stairs into the basement meeting room of St. Matthew's Cathedral in Washington, DC. There was a group of about nine individuals, mostly men, there to greet me. I didn't know what to expect; so as the meeting began, I just sat down and listened. Everyone got a chance to speak and, one by one, they told their stories of how their sexual promiscuity had eventually dominated their lives. Some of the stories were quite encouraging of how lives were being cleansed and renewed, and others were quite sad. Sexual addiction had ruined most of their lives and reputations.

It was encouraging to see how honest these people were. They were very *translucent* with each other. Most were heterosexual; some were homosexual. The group had Christian leanings; however, it was not totally orthodox. I think we ended the meetings with the Lord's Prayer but it was obvious that some of the members weren't Christian.

The group encouraged its members to control our sexual urges; however, its belief system seemed to be contradictory. As far as they were concerned, it was okay to have one gay partner; or, if you were heterosexual, to be co-habitating with one heterosexual partner. This confused me. I was not coming to this group to learn how to *contain* my sin. I really wanted to *heal*. I wanted to be able to have a normal, monogamous, heterosexual marriage. They were teaching us to be "partial sinners" It was bizarre.

However, at the time, it was the best thing available. The group became closer and began to grow. We could share our deepest, darkest secrets with each other. Nobody judged anyone. It was a place to come and vent. God used the SA group to begin to bring me into sexual sobriety. I can't explain it fully; however, something inside me began to change. My daily addiction to masturbation for the last 18 years began to dissipate. I was moving closer towards chastity. My SA peer group was challenging me to say "No" to my deepest darkest sexual urges. After a few months of regular attendance at the group, my mind began to clear, and I actually began to have more of a sexual attraction towards my wife and the rest of the opposite sex.

Part of my recovery from homosexuality and sexual addiction included setting boundaries in my life. I was raised as a Catholic, and in our faith system we are asked to give up something for Lent. Lent is the forty-day period that precedes Easter. In that time we are challenged to give up something of importance to us. The reason this is done is to model Jesus' preparation of his public ministry when "he was driven into the desert" spending 40 days without food while being tempted by Satan.

Where most people give up chocolate or gum for Lent, I decided that abstaining from my addiction to masturbation would be a suitable sacrifice to offer up to God. For some people, giving up masturbation for 40 days and nights might be quite simple. For a sexual addict like myself, this was a major sacrifice. Amazingly, God blessed my Lenten sacrifice. I was able to submit my flesh to the Spirit and, as

Galatians 5:16 promises, "submit yourself to the Holy Spirit and *you will not gratify the sins of the flesh*", that's exactly what happened. I was able to keep my promise to the Lord for the entire 40 days.

Although falling to the sin of masturbation on the 41st day, I noticed that the "thrill" of the act had been greatly diminished. I was angry with myself for giving in to the temptation and not getting the thrill of the act. However it was becoming apparent to me that God was beginning to cleanse me from *all* of my sexual addictions.

I began to praise God in the midst of the SA meetings for another week of sexual sobriety. After four months of sobriety, I began to be amazed. I could not believe what was happening in my life.

The heartfelt joy of what God was doing in my life seemed to irritate the non-believing members of the group. And then one evening, a Christian psychologist *of all people,* **who was a sexual addict himself**, came up to me after my fellow SAers scolded me, and warned me to stop using God's name during the meetings. In a kind way, he was warning me to stick more closely to the SA Manual and guidelines. He then said to me, "It's quite obvious that you're a Christian. It sounds like you don't want to be gay! You know what? You'd be a perfect candidate for ex-gay ministry." I then replied, *"Ex-gay ministry? What's ex-gay ministry?"* He answered, "They are a group of born-again Christians that meet in the Maryland suburbs, on Tuesday nights. **They believe that you aren't born gay and that through the power of Jesus Christ, that you can go straight."**

My eyes widened. I couldn't believe what he was telling me. I immediately asked for details on how to get to their meetings and, on the following Tuesday, I rushed out to the suburbs to a small Presbyterian Church in Maryland. The attendees were a unique bunch. There was a man who was an ex-gay leather biker; an ex-lesbian in military fatigues who was more masculine than me; a Protestant minister who was facing a prison term for trying to molest a teenager; and two quasi-normal looking guys. My first impressions of this group were not favorable.

During the meeting, which was much more biblically-based than the SA meetings, we discussed the Scriptures that forbid homosexual behavior, but at the same time we reviewed other Scriptures that exhorted us to trust in God for healing. The interaction at the first meeting was not monumental; however, I left the church that night feeling a slight glimmer of hope. This group was really a peculiar bunch of people, however just like the SA group, they were *very real* and committed to each other. The man who directed the ministry had been out of the lifestyle for over nine years. His testimony was genuine and encouraging. I began to suppose that maybe I *wasn't* born this way…that maybe I *could* change, and that if *this guy* could do it, maybe I could too!

I was expecting a polished group led by a sophisticated Freudian therapist. To be honest, I was a little disappointed. Immediately following the meeting, I remember crying out to the Lord, after returning to my car, *"Is this how your going to heal me?"* And then I heard Him say "You have asked me for years to free you from homosexuality…and I have provided everything that you will need to heal from homosexuality within this group… **and the rest is up to you!"** I began to weep. I couldn't believe that my prayers were finally being answered. I couldn't believe that God had taken the time to speak to me. It was comforting to know that God even knew that I existed and that He still loved me after all the ways I had disappointed Him.

I raced home on a cloud to break the news to Dianne about how encouraging the meeting was. I was still feeling a bit foolish discussing the more spiritual side of my healing. Dianne wasn't very open to spiritual things at this point in our marriage. I thought she would think that I had lost my mind if I told her *that God spoke to me and said this and that*, so I usually only reported the more tangible effects the meetings were having on me. She wasn't very encouraging either way. Her faith at that time was still young, and I believe that she didn't fully realize what work God was beginning to accomplish in my life and how it would change our lives forever.

I stopped going to the SA meetings because I was receiving much more benefit from the Tuesday night Exodus group. I really was quite annoying at times. Being so excited about my quickly growing faith, I frequently interrupted the group leader with dozens of questions. My faith was becoming alive, and I believe that my zealousness irritated the other members of the group.

The gospel was becoming alive in my life, and the Word of God, filled with its truth, was washing away the time that the locusts had eaten out of my life. The Holy Spirit was taking away my guilt and my shame. God's Word was filling my mind and washing away the memories of a 20-year addiction to pornography, masturbation, and the memories of over 400 sexual partners. Only the Holy Spirit could do that through the Living Word!

One Tuesday night, the group leader announced a regional conference that was being held at a Christian retreat center a few hours from D.C. It was a weekend event and I was very excited to go. Upon arrival, I was astonished to see the condition of this old, neglected Assembly of God retreat center that sat in the hills of Virginia. Can you imagine a narcissistic former-homosexual that was used to the "high life" and staying at the *Plaza Hotel*, spending the weekend at a "tattered" Christian camp ground and sleeping in a dormitory with thirty other homosexuals? And to add insult to injury, we all had to share one bathroom and only one tiny mirror!

One night, during the weekend I remember lying wide-awake on my World War II surplus cot with its saggy old mattress. I couldn't sleep because someone in the next bed was snoring. I remember crying out to God... "You better be in this!" and then after, begrudgingly turning over; I pulled the coarse, *rough-looking* blanket that resembled cheese-cloth over my head, and tried to get some sleep.

I decided to stay and make the best of it. It was kind of intriguing being around 70 ex-gays. I was beginning to realize that I was not *alone*. That this was a *new thing*, a movement of the Holy Spirit that I was privileged to be a part of.

One of the speakers was an ex-lesbian named Starla Allen. The Lord has blessed her with great gifts of healing. That night she prayed over me to be released from more guilt and shame that I carried for being such a promiscuous homosexual. As she and some of the other prayer people laid hands on me, a deep guttural cry came up from the depths of my soul and released me from my shame. I was told afterwards that I had cried for over an hour and that I was sucking my thumb (like a baby). She then informed me that whatever demonic presence had entered my life, had taken a stronghold when I was very young. I was beginning to experience deep inner healing from my bondage.

I felt so much lighter after that weekend and, again, could not believe how wonderful it felt like to revel in the fullness of the Holy Spirit. It was as if spiritual surgery was performed on me. That weekend retreat was pivotal in my healing process and I'm glad that I had had the opportunity to be there.

My wife really began to see changes taking place in my life. They were obvious. And she began to be encouraged by my attendance at these meetings. She knew deep inside of herself that it was important to "release me" to experience this deep inner healing. She never stood in my way, nor did she resent the time that I needed to spend apart from her.

What was an apparent yet simple example that my sexuality was really being repaired was the deeper attraction that was forming inside of me towards my wife. Now that I had made a commitment to be monogamous with her forever – and resigned to that mindset, lying next to her night after night, my desire toward her began to intensify. Our sexual relationship began to improve. It was the equivalent of passing through a very late puberty. My newly awakening attraction to the opposite sex was very exciting. I finally knew what it was like to have *those* feelings. I was becoming heterosexual, maybe 20 years late, but better late than never.

God's timing is always perfect. As all of these changes were going on in my life, Dianne became pregnant with our second child. That January God blessed us with a beautiful healthy baby boy whom we named Carter David. I was now the father of a boy. It was really easy being a dad to Mary Victoria because the feminine in me was over-developed. I don't think that I would have been able to father a boy during the early years of our marriage and before my heterosexual healing had kicked in. Its very hard to pass on your imprimatur of masculinity to your son if you don't possess it first yourself. This masculine maturation was beginning to happen "quick and fast."

This healing was real and permanent - as long as my devotion to the Lord remained. He says, "remain in Me and I will remain in you." Healing from homosexuality is possible for anyone who truly seeks it. God really did hear my prayers and was answering them, but, until I surrendered *totally* to Him, the healing did not come. I had to show Jesus that I was serious and the closer that I moved towards Him, the closer that He moved towards me.

"My brothers, you will always have your trials, but when they come, try to treat them as a happy privilege; you understand that your faith is only put to the test to make you patient, but patience too is to have its practical results so that you will become fully developed, complete, with nothing missing. **If there is anyone of you who needs wisdom, he must ask God who gives to all freely and ungrudgingly; it will be given to him. But he must ask with faith, and no trace of doubt, because a person who doubts is like the waves thrown up in the sea, when the wind drives, that sort of person in two minds, wavering between going different ways, must not expect that the Lord will give him anything." – James 1:2-8 (Jerusalem Bible)**

I began to realize that it had taken many years for me to develop a homosexual disorientation, and that it would take a number of years for my full recovery. But I had crossed over a threshold of hope and I began to feel more and more confident about my new life.

Everybody's healing will be different. No two will be alike; however, we will have many common afflictions that we suffered in our youth that we can overcome together.

The main variables that determine how long the healing process will take include:

- Was there a history of sexual abuse?
- How long did the abuse last? Was it prolonged?
- How early did it start?
- What was the early relationship with the same-sex parent like?
- What was the state of your parents' marriage in the earliest stages of your life?
- Were you teased and/or rejected by your peers?
- (For men) Was your mother overbearing?
- (For women) Was your father (in a non-sexual way) emotionally incestuous?
- Were you exposed to pornography at an early age?

- Was your father or mother psychologically or physically absent in the earliest stages of your life? Did you feel abandoned by either parent?
- Were you molested, raped emotionally or physically abused?
- Were you the victim of incest?
- Was your family dysfunctional? Examples: divorce; drug or alcohol abuse; emotional insecurity; spousal abuse.
- Did you have a low opinion of your father's social position? (Financial depravation may lead to feelings of low self-esteem or inferiority especially if the child is very intelligent and is mixing in with a higher economic group.)
- Were your parents both working and not around enough to nurture you. (Sometimes the homosexual person may have had all the creature comforts of life, such as a cultured high socio-economic background, yet was seen and not heard.)
- (For men) Were you awkward at sports? Example: Were you the last one picked on the softball team?
- (For women) Were you the son your father never had? Were you forced into sports that were more male-oriented to please him or your feminist mother who was using her children to make political statements?
- Did your siblings not include you? Maybe because they were jealous of your intelligence or the attention that was shown to you?
- Were you your opposite-sex parent's (non-sexual) proxy husband/wife?
- (For men) Were you your opposite-sex parent's confidante? Were you told "personal things" constantly about your dad by your mom that was not proper for a young mind to hear? Ex.: He never has sex with me

anymore, or, you understand me more than your dad does.

When considering the above-mentioned variables, it's important to keep in mind that it's the child's *perception* that's crucial to his or her psychosexual development.

I began to realize that many of the experiences that are listed on the last few pages applied to my life. These life experiences or tragedies had affected my psychosexual development. There was no way that they could not have. God began to show me that "the sins of my fathers to the third and fourth generation" had affected who I was as a person or more specifically as a sexual being. The Lord began to show me that I would have to grieve these life experiences. Then He showed me because of what choices others had made for me, and choices that I had made in my adult life, I had developed a homosexual disorientation. This was a **dis**-orientation because this is not the way that the Lord had planned my life to be. He showed me that I was living in a "destiny malaise." In other words my life had taken an alternate course. This was not a course that God intended for my life.

This unfortunately was a course that if I stayed on, would have eventually lead to my physical and spiritual destruction. He would correct it <u>if</u> I were willing to follow him completely and learn to trust Him more. Individuals that have been victims of sexual abuse have a very hard time trusting *anyone*. It was even harder to trust God because I couldn't see Him! I believe that is why God allowed the voice of His Holy Spirit to be so distinctive in my life. Unfortunately, I, like the apostle Thomas, needed to see and hear Him before I believed.

God began to show me that He could not heal me until I forgave the ones who had trespassed against me, (as the Lord's Prayer in the Gospel of Matthew tells us). The Holy Spirit began to show me that my father did not lead me far enough on the road to His Son Jesus through church attendance and His Word. He showed me that although my mother and father really did love me, I couldn't receive their love. One of the ways that He allowed me to experience important healing in my life was to have three good years of relationship with my father before he died of a heart attack at the age of 72. Those three years made up for the 30 unresponsive years that I was estranged from him.

My father retired ten years before he died. I was able to have some wonderful conversations with him before God took him. He sat down with me and took the time to explain to me about the hardships that his family faced when his own father came to this country in 1923 as an Italian immigrant. He told me that during the Great Depression his father couldn't find work and eventually gave up hope. This was very devastating to him, to have his own father believe that he had failed his family.

My dad had to leave school in the sixth grade and shine shoes in downtown Newark, New Jersey just so that his family could continue to have food. He mentioned that it was distressing to him to think that I thought that he was a bad father. From where he came, providing a nice house in the suburbs, staying faithfully married to his wife for 50 years, providing a college education (which he paid for in full), three balanced meals a day and warm stylish clothing was a great accomplishment. I began to fully realize all the sacrifices that he had made for me and how unfairly I had judged him.

He also mentioned that during World War II he was very concerned about being drafted into the army to fight. He was concerned about what would happen to his wife and children if he were killed. He told me that it would be very hard to fight in the war against the Italians especially because he had been born there and most of his family still lived there. The stress of these worries led to a nervous breakdown and he had to be hospitalized for a year in a psychiatric hospital. He also told me that while hospitalized for nearly a year, he was given the Gospel at the mental hospital and that he had read the Bible through three times. He also mentioned that the hospital practiced very experimental electro-shock therapy on him and that although it had helped somewhat, it had changed his entire personality. The four children that were born to him after he was released from the hospital were fathered differently than his first three sons. He was much more emotionally distant from them. I think that it was more than a coincidence that of the last four children that were born after his breakdown; child # 4 became homosexual; child three committed suicide; I was child two and became homosexual for 9 years and my fraternal twin brother became involved with drugs for awhile. (Thank God he later stopped taking them, got married over 26 years ago, and now has a great wife and three children).

He also told me that it was very hard to be married to a woman such as my mother She was very domineering and demanding but at the same time my dad bragged about all the great attributes that she possessed. He mentioned that she was the one who held the family together while he was in the hospital and that she had accomplished many great things that benefited our family. He told me that he loved her and was very content with his life. Then he shocked me and said, "You think Mom and Dad aren't happy, but we really are." As far as he was concerned he had raised 7 children to maturity, had every material comfort he needed and worked hard for 55 years and had 17 grandchildren. He then said that he was very content with life and wished that I were as happy as he was. He told me that he was very proud of me and that he was glad that I had finally grown-up. He also added that he loved my wife and daughter.

Before I let him "off the hook" I shared with him that I had wished that he had spent more time with me. I mentioned that it was very embarrassing to me that mom took me to all the father-son stuff like Cub-Scouts and that I wished that he would have done more with me instead of falling asleep every night in front of the TV. After discussing these issues openly with him, the majority of the anger that I had held towards him dissipated. It was amazing!

The Lord began to show me that I had to begin the process of forgiving all the male predators that had sexually molested me as a child. He began to give me a love for them instead of hatred. He showed me through His Son Jesus that I had been forgiven much and that I should not harbor anger against these people that sinned against me. He showed me that I had seen my salvation and that I should be happy that He saved me and that I should pray for my molesters' salvation. That was very hard but by God's grace, I was able to forgive. Forgiveness is absolutely crucial to the healing process. I would highly recommend that you do a word search on the words forgive and forgiveness in the Bible. It will show you very clearly how important it is in overcoming any life-dominating sin.

It was also important to take responsibility for anything that I had done in my adult life of which I needed to repent. After being gay for 9 years and having over 400 sexual partners, there was a lot for which I needed to repent. I was able to ask a number of people that I had offended or had taken advantage of for forgiveness.

One of the most important healings came when I was able to approach my mother (without harboring anger) and ask her to release me to grow-up. **I literally had to cut the *spiritual apron strings* that were still attached to me. I had to separate from her emotionally**. This was very hard for both of us. She had been my rescuer for many years, and I now had to depend on my heavenly Father to be my rescuer. I also had the opportunity to thank her for all the wonderful things that she had done for me. I really don't think that I would have survived the early years without her maternal comforts. Unfortunately she never let go, and to add insult to injury, *I didn't want her to let go*! In order for me to come into my full masculinity this spiritual break from my mother had to take place.

She tends to try to regress to her Italian-Jewish smothering-mother mode every once in a while; however, now I know how to handle it. I have now been able to cling to my wife and the two of us have become one. It has certainly helped my fathering skills immensely.

I then had to move on to the next stage of healing, which was bonding with other men. This was crucial! I was able to get along fine with women. I had done that all of my life. I now needed to bond with men *without wanting to sleep with them*. I needed to seem them as peers. God was further developing my self-esteem. I didn't have to envy men anymore **because I was one of them all the time. I now know that because my masculinity is intact, I could now see men as my equals even if they were more attractive, more intelligent or more polished.** Praise God!

I had to start bonding with men at church. I needed Godly father-types and brothers in the Lord with whom I could bond. I had to start getting up early on Saturdays and going to the "dreaded" men's pancake breakfast. Yuck! Why church guys do that sort of thing on Saturdays at 7AM is beyond me. When I was in the gay lifestyle I didn't even know that there was a 7 on the clock in the morning! And if we really had to do this male bonding thing, why couldn't we have a men's pancake brunch?

I was a pretty peculiar person. However, I began to realize that I was not very different from the other guys. I wanted to be around them more, and less around women. I also realized that having good taste or a good sense of design...(yes even of the interior type)...was a gift from God and that my talents should be celebrated. I began to become more interested in the more traditionally male things. I learned that wearing clothes that didn't match was O.K. It was a wonderful awakening in my life and I began to relax. I began to feel like "one of the other guys."

One of the last things I experienced that convinced me I was healed was that I was no longer "turned on" by the same sex. The physical arousal had greatly dissipated! One of the ways that God showed me that I was making great progress was by bringing one of the more attractive guys at church into my life. I couldn't believe that he wanted to be my friend. In the residue of my jaded mind I actually believed because he was interested in a friendship with me that he was a closeted gay who was secretly attracted to me. It took my mind a long time to realize that he just genuinely enjoyed my company and wasn't looking for anything in return. We became good friends.

One day I was sharing with him in a men's account-ability group my frustration of still finding men attractive to look at. I then challenged Peter's masculinity and asked him; "when you are in the locker room, do you notice that men are good looking and have good builds? **He answered back very honestly, "Of course! There's nothing wrong with noticing someone is good-looking...but I don't want to sleep with them!"** After hearing his very honest answer, I then knew that I was going to make it!

CHAPTER 9

MY TIME AT EXODUS INTERNATIONAL

In December of 1967, God awakened a lady named Roberta Laurila one night and gave her a prophetic vision of large placards-like billboards, each with the name of a different country. Then in an instant and in the vision Roberta was walking down a long hall peering into different rooms. In each room, there were people talking on phones, counseling those struggling with homosexuality. Roberta was then given a picture of a football stadium, where an evangelist-type person was speaking. The stadium was filled with homosexuals and other people caught in sexual addiction. After an altar call was given, hundreds of homosexuals came forward, seeking God and a way out of the lifestyle. God gave Roberta the message that one day there would be an international network of Christ-centered ministries that would help homosexuals heal.

"If you are willing to leave your lesbianism behind," God said to her, "I will use you mightily." Three weeks later, Roberta left her live-in relationship, and lesbianism, behind forever.

Roberta began to pray daily for God to raise up ex-gays and ministers who knew how to minister to the gay population from all over the world. In the early '70s, the Lord began to rise up ex-gay ministries all over North America and overseas: England, Los Angeles, Holland, South Africa, San Francisco, Minneapolis, and Tulsa. At first, each ex-gay ministry assumed it was the only one in existence; then slowly but surely these ministries discovered that they were not alone. In 1976, an ex-gay group at a church in Anaheim, California called Exit began to network with other ex-gay ministries. In September of that year, the first Exodus National Conference convened. Twelve ministries from across the country met in Anaheim and over 60 participants, mostly men, attended. They didn't know what to call themselves. Remarkably, someone jokingly said, "Let's call ourselves 'God save the Queens.'" However they later agreed that the name Exodus would be more appropriate. A second conference in the summer of 1977 in Oakland, California attracted over 100 participants.

Then the opposition began. The media invaded the conference, and the San Francisco *Examiner* branded Exodus a "fundamentalist, anti-gay organization that uses deprogramming techniques." Most of the media linked Exodus with the Anita Bryant crusade, which was then making national headlines. This spiritual warfare on the founders was exceedingly oppressive. Numerous ministries did not survive the next few years. Outreaches, which had begun in isolation from the mainline churches, were most vulnerable. Without proper financial spiritual and emotional support, some leaders got discouraged and quit. Some leaders who had not fully worked through personal issues had a moral relapse soon after their stories were published. In 1979 at the Johnstown, Pennsylvania conference, there was division within the ranks. One group was moving towards heterosexuality and the possibility of marriage; the other group believed sexual orientation could not be changed, and were moving towards celibacy. The ex-gay movement was young; some leaders were not yet solidly grounded in Scripture, and were making premature opinions based on their personal experience. Exodus took the side of the first camp and stated, "a homosexual orientation was not acceptable or even neutral, temptation is not sin, and a homosexual lifestyle cannot comfortably coexist within a total commitment to Jesus." During the next ten years, Exodus grew slowly but steadily.

I first attended the Philadelphia conference in 1989. There were 400 attendees from around the world. As you would probably guess, ex-gays really know how to put on a conference! Everything, including the choice of setting – Eastern College – was carefully selected. It was a weeklong conference. I had no intention of going to it, but the Lord got me there in a roundabout way. One of the ex-gays who was attending our DC ministry was also a recovering alcoholic. One of his church leaders phoned me one day to let me know they were sponsoring Joe's attendance at the Exodus conference in Philadelphia. They were more concerned that he would have a relapse with alcohol than with homosexuality at the conference, and asked me to accompany him to be his roommate and "keep an eye on him."

I really believed that I was doing a mission of mercy for this kind soul; however, the Lord was actually drawing me to the conference for a continued healing in my own life. I couldn't believe that there were over 400 people like myself whom God was calling out of homosexuality. It was very important for me to see that this was truly a movement of the Holy Spirit. The devil was playing a lot of tricks with my mind when I started the support group in Washington, DC. In my inner thoughts he would speak to me and say, "How ridiculous you are for starting a group like this."… "It's never going to work."… "Don't the 12 of you feel ridiculous?"

However, as I walked into this large auditorium of my first Exodus Conference filled with 400 other people; *also* struggling with unwanted homosexual desires, it was extremely confirming to know that I wasn't losing my mind. It also validated this movement as being truly of God and that He deemed me worthy enough to assist Him in it. He was doing a new thing and on a grand scale: calling the repentant homosexual out of the darkness of the gay world. I had just taken a seat in the auditorium as the opening praise and worship began. It was very Charismatic-Protestant in nature, none of which I was familiar with. However the words to the music were projected onto a large screen and everyone began to sing and freely praise God. It was beautiful! Just about everyone was Spirit-filled and most were raising their hands up to God. I was unacquainted with this style of worship, and it was very unusual but exciting to witness for the first time. I was a Christian at the time, but had not experienced the baptism of the Holy Spirit as described in the bible in the book of Acts, Chapter 2. At first I thought that they were phonies! I wondered why they worshipped in that manner and questioned their sincerity, but as I stared into their faces as they were praising God, I realized that what they were doing was real. It was quite beautiful; they were actually speaking their praises directly to God.

After the music concluded, they announced the first conference speaker whose name was Sy Rogers, the president of Exodus International. As the applause began he approached the stage and took the podium. I noticed very quickly that he was very effeminate and I immediately prejudged him, saying to myself, "If this is the president of Exodus—if this is their best shot—then get me out of here." Even in my "nelliest" days, I was more masculine than he was. What I didn't realize at the time was that the devil was trying to get me to leave the conference and I almost did until an inner voice told me "just to stay and listen to his story."

For an hour or so, he spoke of an incredible story of rejection by his father and his peer group when he was a child. He talked about his very troubled teen years and his walk into cross-dressing and later how he became a pre-op transsexual. He gave explicit details of how he lived as a woman for over 10 years. He talked about the plastic surgery that gave him breasts, high cheekbones and seductive lips. He added that he was basically happy with the lifestyle that he was living. Later, he shared about his two gay male friends that actually "married" each other in Hawaii, and that he had been a part of the ceremony. One day he received a letter from them informing him that they had separated physically from each other, that they had both became born-again Christians, and that they had come to the realization that the gay lifestyle was very much opposed to God's Word, the Bible. Sy found this news very shocking, and he was even more surprised by their closing remark: "and we are now praying that God will call you out of the lifestyle, too."

I was glued to my seat as he continued his story and told the conference participants that this revelation from his friends really began to work on him. He had always presumed that he was gay and that there was not much that could be done about it. Then his testimony became really serious when he began to tell us about a series of supernatural events that occurred when he checked into Johns Hopkins University Hospital in Baltimore for sexual re-assignment surgery. Over the years he had received plastic surgery, taken hormones, and even lived and worked as a woman, however he had never "gone all of the way" and had the "emasculation" surgery. He was very much excited about finally completing his journey from male to female. Pretty soon it would all be over. But one night as he lay in his hospital bed, a few days before the surgery, the Holy Spirit appeared to him as a magnificent light that lit up his room and said 'Sy, do not have this surgery, this is not My desire for your life. If you are willing, I will heal you of your sexual brokenness and use you to bring hope to many others.' Sy couldn't believe what was happening, but he knew it was real. He cried out to God, 'if that was really You, please send me a sign that will confirm your message.' Miraculously, two days later a major press conference was held at Johns Hopkins University Hospital by the Head of the Sexual Reassignment Team, announcing that they were discontinuing all sex-change operations at the hospital because they now believe that they are ineffective. Sy couldn't believe his ears – God had answered his prayer. He checked out of the hospital shortly afterwards and began his healing process by contacting a local ex-gay ministry.

As Sy continued his testimony, it became clear to me why he was still somewhat effeminate in his appearance and mannerisms. I had judged him on his outward appearance and **not** by what God had accomplished on his inside. He truly had been touched by the hand of God and had been transformed. Although his outward appearance showed the scars of his years away from the Lord, his inside, spiritu-ally, was all male and alive with the presence of God. I was extremely humbled and moved by his powerful testimony. The Lord used him to grab my attention that first day of the conference, and I couldn't wait to hear Sy Rogers continue his presentation during the next two keynote addresses.

In gay circles, the "effeminate" guys are looked down upon. The "butch queens," as some of us were called, were more accepted. It made us feel superior to be more masculine appearing on the outside, and some people took great joy in putting down the more effeminate ones. It's the old cliché of "let's step on the weaker ones, so that we can feel better about ourselves," when in reality the more effeminate ones were just more hurt, more damaged or more rejected than we were. It was very sad. In the extreme shallowness in much of the gay world, many of the more masculine gay males had effeminate friends, but were never sexually attracted to them.

There is an unspoken hierarchy of discrimination in the gay male subculture. Masculine-appearing men were at the top, and the transvestites, drag queens and transsexuals were considered the bottom of the barrel. Gay political propagandists tell America, "we love everyone' and 'everyone is included in our rainbow." However, that's far from the truth. Drag queens experienced an enormous amount of rejection by their fellow gay peers, and yet God used a former pre-op transsexual to minister to 400 ex-gays at the conference.

Sy Rogers proved to me that God could use any vessel that He pleases! **This former pre-op transsexual was more of a man than I was, and I earnestly yearned for the inner masculinity that he possessed.** I remember crying out to God that week, "God, if you can heal Sy Rogers, you can certainly heal me," and I praise God for Sy's life. He has shown me very specifically that **being a true man has nothing to do with muscles or a deep voice rather, being a true man is having a sincere relationship with God and living by His Word.** Nothing else will make any difference to God when we come before Him in judgement.

Sy Rogers married a wonderful lady named Karen twenty-four years ago, and they have a beautiful daughter who is now 22 years old and married. Sy and Karen now live in Orlando after living for many years in Singapore and the South Pacific and ministering to many former homosexuals and transsexuals all around the world. God has used their testimony to personally reach thousands of homosexuals for Jesus Christ. He is considered in ex-gay circles to be "an ex-gay minister to ex-gay ministers," and is personally responsible for ministering to the great majority of "third generation ex-gays" that came out of homosexuality in the early 1990's. Sys name is revered in ex-gay circles all over the world. The ex-gay movement would not be where it is today if Sy had not heeded the Lord's call in his hospital room in Baltimore more than twenty years ago. Many people were very sad to hear that Sy and his wife were called to Singapore to spread the ex-gay movement to the Orient, however our loss is their gain. If the Church ever recognizes an ex-gay saint his name will probably be St. Sy of Singapore. God has truly used his testimony in a very important way.

Typically, one might attend his first ex-gay conference with a spirit of doubt and sometimes fear. Many persons who have struggled with homosexuality for sometimes decades will sometimes be carrying a spirit of cynicism. Sy was used by God to put many others and myself at ease at the Exodus conference in Philadelphia in 1989. The Lord had equipped him with excellent communication skills that allowed him to minister effectively to all of the sexually broken people at the conference. He is one of few people that I know who can get you to laugh at yourself while the Lord begins to reveal to you the mess that sin has produced in your life. God delegated Sy to do spiritual surgery on us that week. I am astounded by the amount of healing from past hurts that I experienced in Philadelphia.

Along with Sy's keynote talks, the conference also offered over 60 different workshops on such varied topics as *Overcoming Masturbation*, *Overcoming Anger Towards Parents*, *Freedom from Pornography*, *Addressing Sexual Abuse*, and many others. I was astounded to find that such a conference like this existed! God was answering my prayers through these incredible, extraordinary, and much-needed seminars.

Prior to attending that first national conference, God had begun to heal me from my addiction to masturbation, which had dominated my young adult life. In the midst of my 20-year addiction, I would fall into its grips two or three times *per day*; however, at the time of the conference I was only giving in to the temptation about once a month.

The Lord had convinced me that as long as I persisted with this behavior, I would continue to reinforce my *false* homosexual identity. It had become evident to me that the Big M had to be submitted to the cross. In the next chapter, I will detail how I was healed of this addiction. The class on *Overcoming Masturbation*, taught by Bob Brown at the Exodus conference explained to me so clearly why it violates the proper use of our bodies that I seldom masturbated again. Other than minor temptations, I have now been free from masturbation for over 17 years. Praise God!

Up until this time, I had never experienced God's presence more strongly that at that first conference in Philadelphia. The Holy Spirit was working in a very powerful way. The great majority of the ex-gay men and woman in attendance were very honest and transparent. For me it was the equivalent of being up on the mountaintop in the Father's presence. If you remember the passage in Luke 9: 28-36, Peter didn't want to come down off the mountain after the transfiguration. He wanted to erect tents for Elijah, Moses and Jesus, however the Lord commanded Peter to come off the mountain because he had work for him to do. I knew that it was time to "come off the mountain" and return to Washington. There was work to do! Other gay people needed to hear the *Good News* of freedom from homosexuality.

It was amazing to be there with over 400 people who just didn't feel sorry for what you had experienced in your childhood; they empathized with you because they had been there themselves. We cried together and we laughed with each other. It was wonderful to be in an environment with other gay persons where friendship was more important than a sexual act. This was a group of like-minded Christians (Catholic & Protestant) who just happened to struggle with unwanted same-sex attractions. I no longer saw myself as a homosexual but more so a man made in God's image that had same-sex attraction. The homosexual identity no longer *permeated my being.* I was able to separate myself from my neurosis. *This was major breakthrough in my healing process.*

What was also amazing was to notice the minimal sexual attraction that I had towards the other male conference attendees. There was just one guy that I was feeling uneasy about. His name was Stephen. I couldn't believe it, all week everything was going so well, and then all of a sudden this person shows up and all that had been accomplished that week seemed to go out the window. It was very disconcerting. As much as I tried, I could hardly keep my eyes off him. He was attractive. He spoke beautifully and was very gentle. On top of all this, he began to pursue me as a friend. I wanted to stay as far away from him as possible, but he kept engaging me in conversation.

At night I would cry out to God and blame Him saying, "Why this temptation! I have tried so hard to be good this week. Why must I be tormented in this way?" What I didn't realize was that God had a purpose for bringing Stephen into my life. In my jaded way of thinking I believed that although he was trying to control himself, he was similarly attracted to me. Although he never made any inappropriate gestures to me, this is what the devil had planted in my mind.

The day before the conference concluded Stephen asked me if I would like to play tennis after the afternoon seminars. My motivation for accepting his invitation was not pure. I was becoming emotionally dependent towards him and wanted just be around him even though I knew it was wrong. The tennis game actually turned out to be fun and I stayed within a healthy boundary of friendship.

After the game a group of us met up for dinner. We went on to the evening teaching sessions and afterwards Stephen and I went for a walk alone. I was feeling so convicted to disclose my unhealthy attraction towards him. That's what they taught us at the conference, to be honest and face our fears and on top of that; on the last night of the conference we were all supposed to take Holy Communion together and I was feeling convicted over my unhealthy attraction to him.

The Holy Spirit was really convicting me that I had to tell Stephen the truth—that my desire to have a friendship with him was not totally pure. I felt like I couldn't do it. I was not going to ruin this beautiful male friendship. The kind of friendship I had been craving all of my life —one that was not sexual, but just a regular healthy male-to-male bonded friendship. But I knew that I could not receive Holy Communion in good conscience without confessing my inappropriate attraction.

After walking with Stephen for awhile I stopped and asked him if I could speak with him openly. He said, "Of course!" I stuttered and then finally had the nerve to tell him what was on my mind. I said, "Stephen, as you probably know tomorrow is the last day of the conference, and we will be taking Communion together at the closing service. I cannot do this unless I tell you that I have not had an unhealthy attraction to anyone this whole week, until I met you. I even tried to avoid you, but you have continued to pursue me this week. And I let it happen! And I must confess to you that although I am learning to love you as a friend, my attraction towards you is not entirely sincere." I then began to cry because I thought that this disclosure would end our friendship. But instead of rejecting me, he looked deeply into eyes and said, "Anthony, I knew that you were attracted to me, and I have also been attracted to you *but not in the way you may think*. I love you as a friend—and we will never have sex together—do you understand that?" "Yes, I know that. Now we can be brothers in the Lord! **We can love each other as friends and there's nothing unholy about that.**" He then went on to say he was attracted to me **because of** my personality, my genuineness and my desire to seek God. He also mentioned that I was not even his "type" (which relieved me on one hand and bruised my ego on the other).

He then said, "This is what God desires...men who love each other with an agape love, not an eros love." And then after his comments he surprised me when he put his arms around me and held me close to him for about three minutes. I was able to receive true love from another man without sexualizing it. What was even more remarkable was that after we hugged, the unhealthy attraction that I *had* had for him began to fade. It was awesome!

I had now experienced the kind of agape love that the disciple John displayed towards Jesus at the Last Supper when he laid his head on Jesus' breast. It was poignant and pure. It was the same love that David had for Jonathon - - a pure friendship between two men that was unsullied. Unfortunately, the gay "church" continues to misuse the words of the Bible in an attempt to try to confuse gays into believing that acts of male to male affection that are mentioned in the Bible were actually sexual. This is the farthest thing from the truth.

There are currently four ex-gay networks in the U.S., and of these, Exodus International is based in Orlando, FL. I would like publicly to thank God that Exodus was there for me in 1989 when God called me into healing from my homosexuality. That first conference took me along light-years in my healing process. Exodus has been around since 1976 and has helped lead literally tens of thousands of men and women to healing through the Lord.

Catholics also have their own network that assists the homosexual struggler and teaches him/her how to live according to the teachings of the Church called *Courage*. It has approximately one hundred chapters and is based in New York City.

There is another network within the conservative wing of the Methodist Church that has about forty chapters and is called Transforming Congregations and is based in Bakersfield, CA, and then there is a network called Homosexuals Anonymous that is based in Reading, PA and has about fifty chapters. **(See appendix A for phone numbers, e-mails and addresses for these four networks.)**

Exodus International was very helpful to me and was extremely effective in the 1990's. It is still a great ministry but some of its more recent teachings and leadership need to be challenged. I have found some of their groups to be excellent and some mediocre, so please be aware of this if you decide to be a part of their support network. **However, in my opinion Exodus is the best network out there**.

Please check out the local, chapter of *any* ex-gay ministry that you might think of attending before you submit under their leadership. Some are very good; some are questionable. Sit down with the local director of *any* ex-gay group you are thinking of attending and question their doctrinal stands on the important issues of Christian orthodoxy. Every time the Holy Spirit does a great work such as the Exodus movement the devil will come in and try to water-down their message. My prayer is that this does not happen to *any* of the four ex-gay networks; they are very much needed by the organized body of Christ.

CHAPTER 10

THE BIRTH OF PARENTS & FRIENDS MINISTRIES

⌒◊⌒

I continued to attend my local support group until November of 1988 when the director of the local chapter informed us that he was discontinuing the suburban Maryland meeting, and moving it to a new location in Northern Virginia. The members were quite concerned by this announcement. A few of us who lived in DC had a hard time getting to the meeting on time as it was; the new location would be even farther away and in a different direction entirely. Some members of the group thought this would be an appropriate time to organize a satellite group in downtown Washington. The Lord had given me a burden to reach out to the thousands of gays who lived in the District and the immediate suburbs. It was hard to believe it but at the time downtown Washington didn't have an ex-gay ministry.

We approached the leader of the ministry with our idea. We asked for his blessing on our vision to start a satellite chapter downtown because his proposed new location was not convenient and that maybe we could attract more urban gays to the group. We offered to place the group under his authority. Surprisingly he became very defensive and informed us that he would not support our idea. We were disappointed. We did not have any intention of being disrespectful toward him but he informed us that if we insisted on doing this, that it would be without his blessing.

Reluctantly, we went forward with our plan wishing that we had someone more experienced to assist us. Ron, Wayne and I gathered for prayer one evening and petitioned the Holy Spirit to give us guidance on how to lead and format this relatively new phenomenon: an *ex-gay support group.* That night, He revealed to us, through His word, the steps of recovery that would soon become the ministry Ten-Step Program that could be duplicated anywhere in the country to assist others in restoring their sexual purity. If you don't have an ex-gay support group in the area you can start your own by using the Ten-Step Program that we developed as a model. If you take one step a week in your support group you should be able to meet ten times before you will need additional material. Afterwards I would highly suggest that you contact Homosexuals Anonymous in Reading, Pennsylvania and get their Support Group Workbook. It's one of the best self-help manuals for ex-gays available.

This new ministry was incorporated originally as Transformation Christian Ministries (TCM). Presently it is reorganized as Parents & Friends Ministries (PFM).

Parents & Friends Ministries Ten-Step Program

1. We admit honestly that our homosexuality is sin and that it hurts God and His Son Jesus Christ to know that we are practicing homosexuals: Lev. 18:22, 20:13; Romans 1:24-32; I Corinthians 6:9; Jude 7-8: 1 Timothy 1:8-11 and Galatians 5:18-24

2. We make a decision of our own free will to receive Jesus Christ as our Savior (if we have not already) whereupon the Holy Spirit becomes a part of our

being. John 1:12, 3: 16-18, 16: 7-15; Acts 19: 1-7 and Romans 8:8-11

3. We take an honest inventory of ourselves and make a confession to God by admitting our sins. 1 John 1:5-10; James 5:16 and Psalms 32:5

4. We make a strong effort to read the bible daily and to attend weekly worship services at a full-gospel spirit-filled Church. Exodus 20:8; Deut. 5:12 and Hebrews 10:24-25

5. We truly accept that God can heal us from our homosexuality and that we must have patience and faith to wait for that healing. Romans 12:1-2; Luke 1:37 and I Corinthians 6: 9-11

6. We make a strong effort to rid ourselves of all homosexually-oriented temptations or practices, including masturbation, fantasies, pornographic material, non-supportive friends and frequenting gay cruising areas. Romans 13:11-14; I Corinthians 5: 9-13; Ephesians 4:17-24 & 5:18-24 and Hebrews 12:1-4

7. We seek through prayer and our support meetings to improve our relationship with the Holy Trinity and to pray for power to overcome the temptations of the devil. James 1:2-12; John 8:12 and 2 Corinthians 4: 7-12

8. We will have the strength to overcome the temptations that Satan will use to attack us by calling upon the Holy Spirit and/or calling a Christian friend for help and accountability. Luke 10; 17-20 & 11;24-26 &11:5-10 and I Corinthians 10:12-13

9. If we do have an occasional fall, we will immediately ask for God's forgiveness, turn away from sin and seek God's forgiveness and strength not to repeat the sin. John 8:7-11 & 14:14-18

10. Once through God's grace we have broken the stronghold that Satan had on our lives through homosexu-

ality we will carry the message of hope to others.1 Peter 3:13-17 and Colossians 1:21-29

This ten-step healing program that we developed that night was a combination of the best of the Alcoholics Anonymous (AA) twelve-step recovery program, along with the biblical passages that supported each step. I soon realized that the Alcoholics Anonymous 12 Step Program in its inception was originally based on biblical principles. We condensed the twelve steps down to ten, took the best of the Sexaholics Anonymous (S.A.) program, and combined them with the traditional Catholic understanding of confession and mandatory accountability.

Many Protestants believe that the sacrament of confession is not biblical; however, if one reads James 5:16, it states very clearly, "confess your sins, <u>one to another</u>, and you will be <u>healed</u>!" The Greek word for healed is "therapeuo." That's obviously where the English word therapy is derived from. God's word tells us that **if we confess our sins to each other we will be healed**. We realized what a blessing it was to follow scripture's simple admonition of being transparent with an accountability group of fellow sinners.

Many individuals continue in life-dominating sin as they constantly plead with God to "take the desires away." They continue to fall into cycles of pornography, Internet addiction, masturbation and acting out with other individuals. We soon realized the wisdom in humbling oneself before another believer in the nurturing environment of a support group. Sexual addicts typically need mandatory accountability. We were very excited to know God was using three former homosexuals to begin a ministry that would eventually minister to thousands of homosexuals and their families.

What we found amazing was most churches in downtown Washington, DC would not even open up their doors to a Christ-centered ministry that would reach out to repentant homosexuals. As in most urban cities in America, many of the Christian churches are *spiritually dead*. If we were a pro-gay group, we wouldn't have had a problem finding *room at the inn*. One Episcopal Church at which I inquired was very interested, until they found out that it was an *ex*-gay ministry. Upon realizing what we were really about, the pastor walked me to the door of the church and asked me to leave. It's no wonder that the Episcopal Church is falling apart in America. They have fallen off the authority of Holy Scripture. **How does the Episcopal Church expect a heterosexual male who is struggling with adultery to take advice from a bishop who is co-habitating with his male lover?**

Being so unfamiliar with the matters of church politics, I didn't realize that there were so many apostate congregations in downtown Washington, DC. Back then I really was naive enough to believe that most of the congregations were truly Christ-centered.

I walked into a Disciples of Christ Church that had an interim *female* pastor. Upon realizing the pastor was not a male, this immediately raised red flags in my mind about the spiritual leanings of the congregation. As she began to inquire of my needs, the church secretary walked in. I began to discuss our need for a small meeting room for our ministry that offered support for former homosexuals. As the words former-homosexuals flowed from my mouth, the church secretary walked in and asked, "Would you care for a cup of coffee, Mr. Falzarano?" The disgruntled pastor interrupted her and barked back, "**No, he would not!**" Her secretary's face turned red, and she embarrassingly walked out of the office.

I remarked to her, "I assume by your reaction that you are pro-gay?" She answered, "Yes I am!" I then asked her if the congregation would support *her* doctrinal stand on this issue; she quickly replied, "No, they are an older congregation; they would probably agree with you." I then remarked,

"As their temporary leader, shouldn't you be reflecting the views of the congregation and the Bible instead of your own?"

Wanting to test her orthodoxy a bit more, I then asked, "What are your views on abortion?" She answered, "I am pro abortion!" Her responses were very unbiblical. My soul cringed at her responses. I then "lost it" and rebuked her saying, "The Bible says that in the last days, there will be many false prophets and false teachers who will tell you what you *want* to hear, instead of what you *need* to hear. I can't believe I'm talking to one face-to-face." With that, I walked out of her office, obviously never to be invited back again.

We eventually secured space at St. Augustine's Catholic Church. This wasn't exactly the best neighborhood in town; however, it was the only "manger" being offered.

In fact, it was a rather unsafe neighborhood. I'll never forget when a new man walked into a meeting one night. He showed up late, sat down with the rest of us, and when it was his turn to talk, he began by saying, "When I drove up in front of this church tonight with my new car, I sat out front for a while. One voice whispered in my ear and said, "You don't want to go in there; this is a bad neighborhood," and then another voice quickly chided, "you didn't have any problems going into any gay bars with your new car in even seedier parts of town than this, **now get yourself into the meeting!"**

The first year of ministry had lots of highs and lows. Not having had much expertise in the logistics of running a group made things difficult. We had to depend totally on the Lord to guide us, but our newly christened "ten-step program" carried us through that very tough first year. We also had come to realize the parish that initially welcomed us was rather lukewarm on its stand on homosexuality. It didn't support the traditional Catholic teaching on homosexuality and actually sanctioned homosexual relationships in the congregation. We soon realized that the man acting as the church's evening receptionist was homosexual, and was not happy with our presence. He was cool, uncooperative, and at times openly hostile towards us. When he fully realized what we were really about, he tried to make our Tuesday nights at that church as uncomfortable as possible. Eventually we were asked to give up our meeting space.

The first twelve men who came to the ministry were a unique bunch. Only their common struggle could have brought these twelve people to sit in the same room with each other. The group included a Washington lawyer from a prominent family, a formerly-homeless ex-alcoholic ex-sex addict, an upper middle class businessman from the suburbs, a young congressional aide, a former gay leather biker, a carpenter, a sexually addicted Protestant seminarian, a Catholic priest, and a postal clerk. They represented almost every denomination, race, economic background, and marital status. It was interesting!

Coincidentally, the first parish to welcome us celebrated Saint Augustine as its patron. He lived in the fourth century, at first as a pagan involved in sexual sin of a heterosexual nature for over thirty years before his conversion. After researching his life, I discovered that Augustine also fathered a son out of wedlock. His mother, St. Monica, prayed for her son's deliverance and eventually God granted her request and Augustine repented of his immoral lifestyle. After his conversion he later went on become the Bishop of Hippo (northern Africa) and one of the great doctors of the fourth century Catholic Church. What an interesting coincidence, it seemed that the 'patron saint of sexual purity' was watching over us!

We experienced many blessings in the early days. In the first year, we were fortunate enough to have the prominent psychologist Dr. Elizabeth Moberly lecture at our meeting.

Dr. Moberly is known in ex-gay circles as the "mother of the modern ex-gay movement." Her book <u>Psychogenesis</u>, outlining eight years of research into the origins of the homosexual neurosis, is a classic. Her highly acclaimed book, <u>Homosexuality: A New Christian Ethic</u> is considered to be "the bible of the ex-gay movement". We were also fortunate to have as a guest speaker that year, Jeff Konrad, author of the book <u>You Don't Have to Be Gay</u>. This was one of the first ex-gay books in print in the mid-1980s and still is a best seller. Most ex-gay books (and there are over 100 of them) can be ordered through ha-fs.org or **exodusbooks.org**.

Jeff Konrad came out of homosexuality about four to five years before I did. He has been a role model to many other ex-gays. One time Jeff told me the story that surrounded the publishing of his book. God had put a burden on his heart to compile the highlights of the journal that he kept as he was experiencing his healing process. He also included the highlights of his correspondence with two young men that he helped come out of the gay lifestyle. None of the Christian publishing houses would consider publishing his book in the mid-80s. Jeff felt so strongly that God wanted this book printed that he took $30,000 of his own money to publish the manuscript privately. The book is now in its third printing because of Konrad's obedience to the Lord.

One of the other highlights of that first year of ministry was a phone call that I received from a young cub reporter at the Washington Post. Stephen expressed an interest in coming to cover one of our meetings. He was a very kind, honest reporter and truly interested in covering us. As he left St Augustine's Church that night, he remarked to me, "This meeting was incredible, this movement truly is newsworthy, and it should make a very interesting story." Twelve hours later, he phoned me at the house and announced to me that he wasn't able to do the news piece. I couldn't believe it and asked him why he had been so excited about it last night after he left the meeting? What could have happened to change your mind!' He hemmed and hawed, and then I said, "Just give it to me straight." He answered, "I submitted the story outline to my editor at the Post, and she's a lesbian and she killed the story."

I couldn't believe this lesbian editor actually had the power to kill something that was so newsworthy and important. This was gay politics at its worse. Here we were in the middle of an AIDS epidemic. Gay men, before the miracle "cocktail drugs," were dropping like flies, and this lesbian was killing a story that might have saved thousands of gay person's lives? I began to question who was in control over at the Washington Post. I was beginning to realize that the far-reaching hooks of the gay political lobbyists also extended into newsrooms and television studios all over this country.

I had been a part of the gay world for many many years, but did not fully realize how much it influenced television, Hollywood and journalism. **I soon realized that I was no longer on the politically correct side.** I was quite naïve to think the media and the homosexual community would accept the ex-gay movement. They were <u>not</u> on our side! *My lavender American Express card had been rescinded!* I began to realize that I was now considered a 'turncoat' and the "benefits" that I once enjoyed as part of the gay community were being terminated. I also didn't fully realize that once I started this ministry, I would be coming up against the very powerful well-funded gay political movement in this country. It soon became apparent to me how dangerous I and others like me had become to the gay political agenda in America.

What I also began to figure out quickly was that the ex-gay movement was the biggest threat politically to the pro-gay movement. I was never really a part of their formal movement; however, I learned very quickly that they were moving for gay marriage, gay "civil rights" and "acceptance" of the homosexual lifestyle in the United States. **The ex-gay movement had to be eliminated**. It was too much of a threat! For years they were getting away with *shoving the gay rhetoric down America's throat that gays "were born that way." How were their slick public relations "spin doctors" going to explain 10,000 screaming ex-gays that were healed?*

The gay politicos also did not appreciate my being very public about what *really* goes on in the gay sub-culture. These public revelations would throw a monkey wrench into their highly developed propaganda campaign.

For years the gay politicos had been lobbying the federal, state and local governments with deception data concerning the origins of homosexuality. After their successful manipulation of the American Psychiatric Association, they were now moving towards the repealing of sodomy laws, adding sexual orientation to existing civil rights laws classifications, and the destruction of the traditional Judeo-Christian values concerning morality in American culture. Here comes a person that God has called out of homosexuality and has healed throwing a monkey wrench into the slick Rolls Royce engine of the pro-gay political machine.

This was a movement of God that the gay activists were not prepared for. In their new "revisionist strategy," the ex-gay movement must either be ignored with the hopes it will go away, or it must be attacked, slandered, and discredited in the hopes it can be neutralized. Anyone standing in the way of the very powerful gay political movement must be taken out. Fifteen years later, I know understand why my family and the ministry that I have founded have been under such terrible spiritual attack for entering the "public arena." I now know why God has asked my life to be so "squeaky-clean" with every "I" dotted and every "T" crossed. God was showing me that just about every move that I would make would be scrutinized. And if He were going to use me for

His glory, everything that was not of Him would have to be purged from my soul.

Around that time a reporter from the Washington City Paper, one of the more liberal papers in the nation's capital, called and wanted to do a story about the ministry. Her name is Kate Boo and in my opinion was a well-balanced journalist who thought our story was newsworthy. Although her leanings were to the center, I believed that she was young enough not to have been *affected* yet by the liberal journalistic world.

She wanted to do a straightforward story about the ex-gay movement. She had gay friends; therefore she was not naive about the dangers of the gay lifestyle. It was the late 1980s, many of the readers of the City Paper were gay, and the AIDS epidemic was devastating the homosexual population. This would be a very timely story and a very appropriate venue for *The City Paper.*

Kate came out one night and covered the meeting and afterwards published an extensive front-page story that was fair and balanced. Many employees at the *City Paper* were gay and tried to dissuade Kate from publishing the story, but she was determined to follow it through. It became very obvious to Miss Boo that she was unearthing a "time bomb" of a topic. This was a major article in which the paper even invested in some original artwork for the front-page.

The gay community reacted towards it and was livid. They were not interested in hearing about Kate's honest observations of her coverage of Transformation Christian Ministries. Miss Boo called me right after the article was published and told me that the responses that were coming in were really heated. The article also triggered the greatest number of *Letters to the Editor* in the paper's history. Our phones began to ring off the hook. Surprisingly, many of the phone calls were favorable.

Gay men and women who wanted "out of the lifestyle" began to contact us and the ministry began to flourish. It was time to "come out of the ex-gay closet" or, as I've heard it said, **"It's time to go back into the closet and come out the front door."** The world needed to know that God loves homosexuals, and wanted to heal them. The Lord was beginning to ask the leaders in the ex-gay movement to drop their nets into the water and get ready for a harvest. It was a very frightening, but exciting, time.

Finally, all I had been through had not been in vain. God was beginning to validate the vision that He had asked me to carry out. The sheep were finally coming in, and it was time for this buckaroo to open the corral gates!

CHAPTER 11

THE WAR STORIES: THE SUCCESSES AND FAILURES

I'd be deceiving you if I said that everything in the formative years of the ministry was *ginger-peachy*. If I had known what I was getting myself into years ago, I probably would have never accepted this call on my life. When I told the Lord that I would "go for Him" as the prophet Isaiah did, I didn't fully realize how tough this call would be.

Once you come out of homosexuality and start living your life from the heterosexual mindset, you begin to realize fully just how narcissistic the typical gay person can be. The pendulum in my life swung from the far left to the far right for a while. I actually began to realize that **for a short time**, I had become a bit homophobic and intolerant. Especially when I began to realize the distinction between the average homosexual who just wanted to be left alone versus the pro-gay lobbyist/activist who had a power agenda.

These activists were using the unfortunate circumstances of the AIDS epidemic and putting a PC spin on it and then using it to acquire funds to fuel the biggest gay propaganda campaign in American history. In essence homosexuals who have been victimized enough by society **where now were being re-victimized by their own kind!**

My righteous anger was directed at the gay activists and health officials who refused to close down the gay bathhouses even though they knew that AIDS was spreading through gay America and now the rest of the world. On top of that, the Mafia operated many of the back-room bars and bathhouses where greed clouded their conscience. They didn't really care if the gays died. Could one really expect the mob and the liberally controlled city governments to do *the right thing;* to act responsibly and shut these places down? The organized gay political community was unwilling to shut down the gay sex establishments because in essence they would be admitting that they were the propagators of the AIDS epidemic and they were disinclined to "fess-up" and take responsibility. May God have mercy on these people in power who were responsible for keeping America **and** the misinformed homosexual community in darkness.

The Stubborn Lambs

Ministering to a former homosexual or lesbian could be quite time-consuming and sometimes slow moving. Learning patience in this area did not come easily. As I ministered to them, I sometimes was impatient with their personal healing process. God had to remind me, *quite often,* of the great patience He had with me as I was healing from my own brokenness. Then in remembering how much mercy God had shown me concerning my former lifestyle, I was able eventually to become a more effective minister. I would often question God: "Why me? Why did you allow me to become homosexual? Why did you call me out of it? Why did you save me from death? You allowed Fred, my former boyfriend, to die of AIDS when he only had sex with three people in his entire life. I have had sexual relations with over

400 people, yet you spared my life, and I am HIV negative?" The Bible answered my question as I read in Romans 9:20-22 about questioning the Lord's ways where it says, "Who are you to question, O man, my ways? Shall what is formed say to Him who formed it, 'Why did you make me like this?' Does not the potter have the right to make out of the same lump of clay some pottery for noble purposes and some for common use?"

Another understanding that I received from the Lord went something like this, "Anthony, you knew that you were a sinner. I knew the inner thoughts of your heart. And I knew that you would respond to my call of salvation."

A deep sense told me that I had had a conversion similar to St. Paul's. St. Paul deserved to be burning in the bluest flames of hell. He was persecuting and killing the early Christians. Instead of zapping him, God decided to save him to show the world the depth of His grace and desire that no one perish. St. Paul eloquently alludes to this in I Corinthians 15:9-11 when he says, "I am the least of the apostles, and do not even deserve to be called an apostle, because I persecuted the church of God. But by the grace of God, I am what I am, and his grace to me was not without effect. No, I worked harder than all of them – yet, not I, but the grace of God that was with me."

Chrissy

The Lord began to soften me. He gave me a great amount of patience, endurance, and a special dispensation of His mercy to share with some of the most hardened gays that I had ever met. One person that comes to mind is Chrissy. She came to TCM via the City Paper article. She was in her early 20s and was a very hardened lesbian whose very co-dependent lover had just committed suicide because she, Chrissy, had left her. She was really hurting and mourning the loss of her friend even though she knew that she had had to end the relationship because it was *sucking the very lifeblood out of her.* So when she read about us in the City Paper article that Kate Boo wrote she called me immediately because she needed a support group. She showed up at the meeting one night. She was the first lesbian to start coming to the group. On the surface, her large frame gave her an imposing presence. She was very bossy! And yet, as she and I became acquainted and she trusted me with her story, my spiritual eyes began to see her true image, that of a fragile, delicate young girl.

Most lesbians are not promiscuous, but Chrissy was. She was doing exceptionally well in the ministry. She was four to five months clean from sexually acting out. One day, she came up to me and said, 'I'm very excited about what's happening in my life. I was raised Catholic and would like to go see a priest.' I didn't know many Catholic priests or Protestant ministers because Dianne and I were relatively new in town, so I referred her to a priest at a local parish in downtown Washington. The next day, I called her and asked her, "What did you think of the priest I referred you to?" She paused on the phone and then answered, "You're not going to like this, but he is gay himself, and he gave me pro-gay theology materials to read." I was devastated.

God was beginning to show me that there were quite a few "wolves in sheep's clothing" in the Catholic/Protestant clerical circles. I had to be very careful to whom I made referrals. Chrissy began to listen earnestly to this young apostate priest's pro-gay deceptions, and she eventually returned to the gay lifestyle. She took a new lover and they decided they wanted to have children. Chrissy being the more 'butch' one convinced her lover to carry the baby. They had a serious argument during the pregnancy. The lover, knowing that Chrissy was at least nominally Christian and against abortion, tried to manipulate her into staying with her. And when she didn't, she threatened to abort the baby. Chrissy literally had to beg the woman to carry the baby (that turned out to be twins!) to term. Shortly after the twins were born, Chrissy came home from work one day and on the front porch of her home were two wicker baskets. Her ex-lover literally dropped the babies off with a note reading, "**Dear Chrissy, you wanted *these*; you take care of them. I'm out of here**!"

Chrissy tried to do the right thing by raising the children. As a practicing lesbian, the pressure was too much. She later became involved with drugs, contracted AIDS and had to give up the custody of children to her parents before she died. I had had such high hopes for her! I really believed that she was going to make it. This is what happens when you turn away from the word of God, or listen to false teachers who "tell you what your itching ears *want* to hear, vs. what you *need* to hear."

ARNOLD

Another horror story was Arnold. A Catholic priest had molested him when he was a teenager. He came from a rough background and was reared in a dysfunctional family. He came to the ministry in the early years. He was doing exceptionally well at PFM when one day he called and asked If I could refer him to a Catholic priest. Obviously, I was not going to refer him to the same priest who had led Chrissy astray, so this time I referred him to the Archdiocese of Washington's official Liaison to the Gay Community for counseling. The priest's name was Rev. John Gingrich. Arnold went over to the Cathedral a few days later to meet with him.

During the 'counseling session" Gingrich asked Arnold what his hobbies were, Arnold told him he liked to sing. Knowing this, the priest proceeded to give him instructions on how to contact the Gay Men's Choir. Arnold began to become quite suspicious about the priest's motivations and agenda. He knew that something was not kosher, so when the priest in his next move tried to seduce him, Arnold wasn't very surprised. Thank God the priest was not successful, Arnold was able to shun his advances and leave the rectory. However when Arnold returned home he called me in tears; telling me that he was angry with God. Here he was, trying to go straight, struggling with the results of his molestation by a priest when he was a young adult, and now he's been re-victimized by another priest. I contacted the chancellor's office to report this abusive incident to the offending priest's superiors. The chancellor asked Arnold to submit a written account of the situation and mail it to him. After he had received it and read it, he told us that he would contact us for a hearing. He eventually called and arranged a meeting. Arnold was young and scared. He needed someone there to support him as he confronted his abuser. At first the chancellor wouldn't allow me to attend the meeting, but we insisted! We told him that if he didn't allow **both** of us to attend, we would contact the media! He relented, and I was allowed to accompany him to the hearing. The priest (who had tried to seduce Arnold) was in his early 70s, did his best to deny the charges, and that infuriated us even more.

Arnold began to tell the chancellor the story of how suspicious he was of the priest's intentions when he proceeded to hug him for three solid minutes His suspicions were eventually validated when he kissed him on the mouth right in the Cathedral rectory. What was even more alarming was when the chancellor began to spin the story and started to accuse Arnold of being the perpetrator of the incident! The chancellor then said, "Are you sure that he wasn't just trying to console you while he was hugging you?" At that point, although I wasn't supposed to speak during the inquiry, I lost it and yelled out, "For Pete's sake, he stuck his tongue in his mouth! Is there any question in your mind what has transpired here? This outrageous behavior must stop. These actions drag the Lord's Name through the mud when one of His ministers abuses his authority."

I then turned to the elderly priest and said, "Arnold is getting help for his problems. We are here today not to cause trouble for you or the Church, but to make sure that *you* get help for *your* problem, and that you never, ever do this again. Now if you would just admit your guilt and promise to get some help, and if the chancellor will assure us that you will step down from your position as Liaison to the Gay Community for the Archdiocese, we will consider this issue settled effective immediately. I believe that the Holy Spirit has sent us here to warn you to stop this atrocious behavior and get some help, because someday you will be accountable to God."

We then hugged the elderly priest and left the chancellor's office. Just when I thought this whole ugly episode was settled, something inside me prompted me to call the Cathedral the following week. When the church secretary answered the phone I informed her that I was struggling with unwanted homosexual attractions and needed some help! She then said, *"May I put you on hold while I connect you with Father Gingrich?"* I wanted to scream! I couldn't believe it. I hung up the phone immediately and called the chancellor. When they connected me to him I just blasted him for his arrogance and said, "If you don't relieve Rev. Gingrich from his position today, we will go directly to the Washington Post!" Then and only then was Gingrich removed from his position.

The Lord used me in a more timely manner than I realized; six months later, I picked up a copy of the gay weekly newspaper, *The Washington Blade*, and read the headline in shock and disbelief: REV. JOHN GINGRICH *LIAISON TO THE GAY COMMUNITY FROM THE ARCHDIOCESE OF WASHINGTON DIES IN HIS SLEEP*. My soul grieved for this man. I pray that he had repented for his behavior before he died.

That was it for me. Any hopes of staying in the Catholic Church "and trying to reform it from within" were dashed! My wife and I finally decided that it was time to leave the Catholic Church behind and head over to a Christ-centered Spirit-filled non-denominational Church.

BARNEY

For every Chrissy or Arnold that doesn't make it out of the lifestyle, there is a Barney who does. Barney was one of the "toughest cookies" that Transformation has ever ministered to. He was literally dragged to our weekly meeting one evening by a well-intentioned Christian couple that wanted very much to help him.

Barney was quite a character. He was very personable and polite. He seemed to be in his late 50's and was a real southern gentleman. I presumed that he had enjoyed the meeting; however, afterwards he informed me that he didn't have an interest in leaving the lifestyle behind. "It's too late for me," he said, "I've been in the lifestyle for almost 40 years!" I told him that it was never too late and that no one could force him to come here, but that he was welcome anytime. I selfishly asked him if he would keep in touch because I was interested in hearing his anecdotes of being a part of the early gay subculture of Washington, DC. Although he wouldn't commit to coming to the meetings regularly, he told me that he would phone.

When he would call or we would get together, I loved hearing his stories about the early Washington gay subculture. He was a walking journal of gay political history and trivia of the nation's capital. Barney was employed as a butler for a very prominent Washington hostess on Embassy Row who used to entertain many of the politically elite from the Kennedy through the Bush administrations.

We would drive around Washington, and suddenly he would point his finger and say things like, "There used to be a gay bar on that corner," or, "That park used to be a gay meeting area."

Although Barney was quite an incredible storyteller, he would seldom allude to his "dark side" — the side of him that led him down the road into the gay subculture of the late 1950's, alcoholism and later promiscuous behavior. The Lord put an incredible burden on my heart for Barney. I really wanted to see him make it; however, his commitment to Jesus seemed to be almost non-existent. His faith was very weak, and he was just a child inside who was very scared to step out on ex-gay waters. After awhile his phone calls became more infrequent and eventually they stopped.

In the early years of the ministry I thought if we lost someone back to the subculture, that it was forever. I didn't realize that God in His wisdom and grace would allow certain people back after they've learned the hard way that the gay lifestyle eventually leads to a dead end. And then after not hearing from Barney for a few years, that's exactly what happened. He called the office one day, my assistant handed me the phone, and said there's a guy named Barney who wants to speak to you. I was excited to hear from him after such a long time but was saddened to hear what he had to say. He could hardly talk, but he told me that he was in the hospital and that he was dying of AIDS. He was terribly scared and asked me if I would come over to the hospital and see him. I told him that I would be right over, grabbed Brenda (my assistant) quickly briefed her and off we flew to the Washington Hospital Center.

The effect of the AIDS epidemic was really hitting Washington in a big way in the early 90's. I had lost contact with my gay friends from my former life and had very little exposure to people who were in the last stages of this dreaded disease. It was shocking to see Barney in this state, however

God gave me great peace to handle the situation. As Brenda and I entered his room we really had to do our best to remain composed. Barney looked terrible. This man that I had known as a meticulous well-groomed older gentleman was lying in his hospital bed in an emaciated state, with greasy hair (that probably hadn't been washed in a week). Trays of uneaten food were carelessly left in his room. The lights were out and the curtain on the only window in the room was drawn. No one had even taken the time to shave him. He was such a vain man. If he had seen what he looked like in the mirror, this alone would have killed him.

I tapped on his shoulder bringing him into consciousness and held on to his hand. Until I received his telephone call, I didn't even know that he was HIV positive. I felt helpless. I didn't know what to do. And then by the Holy Spirit's guidance I was prompted to take action. I switched on the lights in his room, opened the curtains and then the window so that some fresh air could wash away the staleness of the room. Next I grabbed some of the food *that was still edible* from one of the hospital trays and begin to feed him.

It was obvious that the hospital had just given up on him and was waiting for him to die. He was literally being starved to death. It was a rude awakening to see how callously some of the early AIDS patients were treated. We gave him an orange to suck, which introduced some vitamin C to his body so that he could handle the stress on his system, plus some additional liquids for the dehydration. We took a cool damp washcloth to bring some comfort to his face. I borrowed scissors from one of the nurses and began to trim his hair. I was then able to locate a shaving razor and after applying some lather, I began to shave Barney's beard. I had never taken care of the physical needs of an AIDS patient and really didn't know how communicative the HIV virus was, so I donned some latex gloves as a precaution and half- way through the shave "nipped" him with the razor. Blood spilled out all over my hands. For a second I froze… mortified at the thought that I had touched HIV infected blood. I quickly cried out to God, (under my breath)…please watch over me and protect me! The fear quickly left and then I knew that there was no turning back now…if this is my calling… I will take care of gay people… no matter what the consequences!

After Brenda and I prayed for him I turned to him and said, "Now Barney, get out of that bed…God is not through with you yet!" And guess what? That's just what he did! Fifteen years later, Barney is still with us. I don't think wedding bells are in the plans for his life; however, I can't tell you how much God has used him as a role model for the younger members of this ministry. He has been clean from acting out for over eight years after a lifetime of sexual promiscuity involving hundreds of anonymous partners.

Barney has also overcome a lifelong addiction to alcohol after attending a Christian based, AA-type program in Northern Virginia. As I mentioned earlier, Barney was one of the most obstinate individuals that I had ever ministered to mainly because he was dealing with early abandonment issues and had been in the lifestyle for nearly forty years. His mother died while giving birth to him, and a father, who was deeply wounded by his wife's untimely death, raised him. His father's parents helped raise him, but Barney really needed the love and attention of his father who had abandoned him psychologically while burying his grief in his farm work. The young boy hung out with grandma and his aunt all the time and soon became a "mama's boy" while also suffering a rejection from his male peer group.

He was obviously very ambivalent towards us. He would sometimes exhibit a classic textbook example of "transferred defensive-detachment" as he would continually thank the ministry for all they had done for him. And then the next day his personality would turn and he would call us on the phone in a drunken stupor and curse us out calling us phony Christians.

Some nights at the meetings he would cheer everyone up and encourage them in their healing process and then by the end of the night he would lose his temper...and then tell us he was going out to have sex. It was a constant roller coaster ride. When his nice personality was dominant he was so sweet that you wanted to just hug him and then in a second you would want just to wring his neck!

Finally I couldn't take it anymore and felt that it was time to give Barney an ultimatum, either shape up or ship out. He had pushed the entire ministry staff to the edge. And one night it all came to a head while the ministry was hosting a social function at a local restaurant in the suburbs of Virginia. A group of about fourteen decided to meet at a nice restaurant for dinner. Life at the ministry had been a bit hectic, and Dianne and I thought it would be a good idea to join everyone.

It started out to be a wonderful evening. The food, the conversation, the music; everything was just perfect until Barney decided he wasn't getting enough attention. He stood up, grandstanded and announced that he was going to the bar to get a drink. Ordinarily that's all that he would have to do to quiet the room so that all attention was on him. One of the ministry leaders who happened to be his roommate turned to me and whispered, "You've got to stop him," when a little voice in my head said, "No, let him go if he wants; it's time for Barney to grow-up!" So I told Barney that we were sick and tired of his manipulation and that if he wanted to get drunk that we were not going to stop him anymore! He defiantly walked away from the dinner group and headed for the bar. I felt that it was important to follow my instinct and just to let him be.

He returned to the table five minutes later carrying what seemed to be triple vodka. I couldn't believe how much he was acting like a spoiled brat, however we all decided to ignore him. We finished our desserts, paid the bill and started to head for our cars. Barney originally rode with Dianne and me, and as he walked up to my car and started to get in, I stopped him and said, "Barney you are not welcome in my car in your drunken state. You can either walk or take a cab home!" He retaliated by beginning to abuse us verbally and to swear at us in the middle of the parking lot with statements such as, "you f—ing phony Christians. I'm going to the bars tonight and back into the lifestyle, etc, etc." Although we loved him dearly, it took all the strength we had in us, to ignore his abuse and drive off leaving him in the parking lot of the restaurant. A few of us were concerned about his safety, so we prayed that God would bring him home without harm and "to his senses."

We all returned to Barney's roommate Steve's home to have a Bible study and ten minutes later the door slammed open and in walks Barney complaining that he had to pay ten bucks for a cab home. He was really trying to put a guilt trip on us ...but we wouldn't have it. Then he picked up the portable phone within earshot of all of us and decided to call one of his gay-friendly buddies to let him know how cruel we were. Then when he realized that we were no longer buying into his manipulations, he stomped up stairs to his room. We became very quiet. We didn't want him to go to the gay bar that night so we decided to pray for him. Shortly thereafter I heard him crying and decided to see if he was all right.

I quickly ran up to his room and asked him if we could talk. He said yes, so I began to plead my case with him. I said, "Barney you have so many gifts to offer. We have done everything within our power with the limited resources that this ministry has to offer to help you, but I am here to tell you that we can't take anymore...that we are frustrated and exhausted. We can't stop you from drinking or tolerate your threats to return to the lifestyle any longer. We love you very much and you know it. However, I think that we have been enabling your behavior and it's really not in anybody's best interest to continue like this." And then he really surprised me, turned to me and said, "I know that all of you have gone out of your way to help me and I have really been a real jerk! I just can't believe that you left me at the restaurant." I said, "Barney we are serious. You either have to sink or swim!" He then looked me in the eyes and began to cry and said, "I'm so sorry that I have caused you, your family and the ministry so much grief...I'm really sorry and I really want to change my behavior...please don't give up on me!"

I then began to hug him very close as he began to weep in my arms. After he quieted down, I told him that he should go downstairs and apologize for ruining everybody else's night...he said that he would do it. Barney walked downstairs and asked everyone's forgiveness. He began to mature that night.

This is what we have to go through sometimes to break someone of his really unhealthy behavior. It takes inner wisdom, courage, and sometimes every ounce of energy that you have left in your body. Barney had a few more minor episodes from that time on, but that night he turned a corner that was remarkable. After we "spanked his inner child" for the last time something inside clicked and he began to grow from a boy into a man and was able to see that we truly loved him. He was able to receive the tough love that enabled him to be set free from his bondage to men and alcohol and has become a source of strength for many people in this ministry.

God was beginning to show me that some of the people that I would be ministering to were people with AIDS. I would have to receive some formal training and education on the subject if I were going to be effective in helping them and at the same time protect myself from risk of infection.

There was an awful lot of unawareness out there in the early 90's that could have been overcome with basic education on this subject. The pro-gay community is doing a better job of reaching out to the AIDS community then the Church is...this must change! I remember my own church group turning down our request to have a simple bake sale so that some of the members of our support group would be able to go to our annual national ex-gay conference. They were actually worried that the whole congregation would catch AIDS from the brownies and cupcakes! That infuriated me, especially since we had a medical doctor on our church board. He was a well-known AIDS researcher who could have easily educated the parishioners on any risk involved.

CONSTANTINE

Constantine was an attractive former street-prostitute in his late twenties who just showed up at my office one day. He seemed to have everything going for him. He told me that he had been born again and wanted to walk out of homosexuality. I told him that I would help him. He was extremely immature for his age; he acted like a young teenager. As a young teenager he became involved in drugs and eventually was forced to leave his home by his parents because his addiction was destroying their family life.

After giving me the gruesome details of his life on the street as a prostitute, he then begged me to help him. He said that he had to get his life in order and make things right with his family because he was dying of AIDS.

This was the first person that came to the ministry that not only needed spiritual care for his sexual dysfunction, but also needed medical care for his HIV infection. I had lost over forty friends to AIDS and three former boyfriends, but had never had to be the primary caregiver to an AIDS victim.

He lived about 2 ½ more years. He was in and out of the hospital constantly with pneumocystis. Because he did not have medical insurance, he received publicly funded medical care. His youthful, muscular frame literally deteriorated before our eyes. It was a horrible death. He was so scared and so alone. As he was approaching the end, I contacted his family in North Carolina. There was a wonderful reconciliation with his dad and siblings before he died.

At that time, there were about thirty of us in the ministry. We all took turns at the very end trying to make him as comfortable as possible. One Friday night, shortly before he died, we were all heading up to an ex-gay regional retreat. It was very hard for us to leave him alone that weekend. When we returned home Sunday night, a group of us came to visit him at the hospital. As we walked into his room, we noticed the lights were off and curtains were drawn. There were trays of uneaten food all around the room and Constantine was groaning. I said, "Constantine, haven't they been taking care of you this weekend?" They had decided that he was taking a turn for the worse and while we were gone that weekend, they neglected him and basically left him to die.

We switched on the lights; we gave him some fluids. He was dehydrated and sucked down two cups of water with a straw. We fed him, prayed with him and made him as comfortable as possible. He made it through the night. The next day I asked the hospital for an accounting of their negligence. They had no answer. Constantine rebounded and lived six months after that. His immediate family was very helpful in the last few months. We were all there when the Lord took him. The family was kind enough to have the body prepared by a local funeral director so that we could say a proper goodbye. It was a beautiful funeral service. The Holy Spirit's presence was all over it and then the body was transported back to North Carolina for burial.

MICHAEL/TERESA

One of the most hardened individuals that I ever ministered to also had the most heart-wrenching testimony that I had ever come across in eighteen years of ministry to the repentant homosexual. My wife and I lived in a transitional neighborhood in downtown Washington. The pre-op transsexual prostitutes used to "sell themselves" on the streets of our neighborhood at night. The police commonly call them "he-shes." They were men dressed as women. There were dozens of them roaming the streets, night after night, selling themselves so that they could support their cocaine habit. Most of them were black, but this one guy was white, so he in particular stood out.

One peculiar thing about this particular "he-she" was that although most of his fellow prostitutes wore wigs, he had allowed his hair to grow long and bleached it blonde. He wore tasteful little outfits; many of them that he designed himself. Although I'd witnessed to many of the pre-op transsexuals on several occasions, for some reason, God gave me a special concern for him. He used to hang out in front of our home at night, in order to irritate us. Whenever he would "work the corner" in front of my house, it would increase the "john" traffic which, of course, would keep my family and me awake at night. He knew what we were all about and tried to "annoy us" out of the neighborhood.

One morning around 3:00 AM, I could no longer sleep because of the "ruckus" outside and went downstairs to have a "chat" with Terry. He noticed me coming out of the house. I said hello to him and he returned the greeting. He then said, "You're that *ex-gay preacher* everybody's been talking about." I asked him his name. He said his name was Teresa. Then I asked, "What's your *real* name?" He was taken aback by that question, paused, and then said, "I don't tell anybody that." I responded with, "I'm not going to address you by your street name or "girl name"... What's your *boy* name?" He realized that I knew how to communicate in street language. He then answered, "My name is Michael." I then said, "Michael, how did you end up out here? I was gay for nine years, but never really understood why some gay men like to dress as women." Surprisingly, he then said that if I wanted to hear his story, now was not the time, but if I wanted to talk, he'd come by later during the day.

When we finally did meet, we sat down together and he began to tell me his story. He told me his mother and father never married. "When my mother was pregnant with me, my father *split*. My mother was a serious alcoholic and later became addicted to drugs. She had many boyfriends. One of them was a child molester. When my mother would leave during the day, looking for drugs, this man would rape me, beginning when I was four. When my mother broke up with him, to punish her, he kidnapped me when I was six years old and locked me in a basement with no windows for six months. Once a day, he would unbolt the door to feed me and if I didn't drink my milk, he'd throw it in my face." I knew that he was telling the truth. The story was so heavy that I couldn't handle it! I began to weep. He stopped speaking for a while and we hugged for a while and then he continued his story. I knew that I had a slightly abnormal family background, but this stretched the parameters of my definition of what constituted a dysfunctional family. It helped me put into perspective just how normal my upbringing had been in relation to Michael's.

He had been living on the streets by the time he was 11 years old. He said he felt so ugly inside that dressing up in women's clothes made him feel pretty. Michael went on to tell me that he had never had any healthy male role models in his life and the men that had been in his life were either alcoholics, drug addicts and/or child molesters.

Obviously his masculinity had never developed. He was 27 years old, but looked much older. He began to dress up as a woman in his early teens, lived mainly in vacant houses and prostituted himself, sometimes six to eight times a night in order to buy the strongest drugs that his body could tolerate. The drugs anesthetized the horrible nightmare called childhood. We hugged each other and cried again and I told him that I loved him, and that if he was willing, he could turn his life over to Christ. He said he'd have to think about it. A few months later, just when I thought that all the conversations with Michael were in vain, he showed up at our home after he'd been beaten up by a "trick," and said, "I've had enough." He said that he believed the drugs that he had taken for so many years had destroyed his mind. He also believed that the demons from the thousands of men with whom he'd had sex with would never let him go. He came to live at our ex-gay live-in program that we'd started at Logan Circle in Washington, However he only lasted two months before returning to the streets. We were not equipped to handle his addiction to drugs and alcohol. We did some research into a Christian drug rehab house in New Jersey where he could live free of charge as he de-toxed. We believed that he had to leave Washington DC because there were over 15 years of familiar haunts that were too much of a temptation for him. He refused to go to rehab, and, with great pain, after he kept sneaking out at night to sell himself in order to feed his continuing drug addiction, we had no choice but to ask him to leave.

Michael lasted a few more years on the streets. He eventually died of AIDS. It was sad to see him, at the very end, walking around the "old beat," with his legs and feet bloated from complications from HIV infection, in high heels, trying to look sexy and, surprisingly, still being able to attract "business." (Sic)

MIKE

Then came some of the great ministry success stories. There was a gentleman named Mike who came to the ministry when we had first started. He was in his early twenties, attractive, struggling with homosexual temptations. However, he never acted upon them and remained a virgin. He was one of the most faithful members of the ministry. He volunteered his free time to the ministry in the early days when we didn't have the funds to hire permanent staff. Although Mike was still a virgin, some of the men that have never acted out were sometimes the toughest to minister to. They are sometimes persuaded by the devil to believe that they are missing something. They in some instances are sometimes envious of those in the group who have "been around the block."

He had been attending the group and was doing extremely well. One summer afternoon, he came over to my house in an angry mood, demanding to talk with me. We went out to sit in front of my house. I didn't know what was on his mind until he began to cut into me verbally. He began to tell me that the temptations were so bad that he couldn't take it any more and that he was giving up!

Mike then told me that he had never experienced the lifestyle and that he was jealous of the other guys in the group who'd had an opportunity to taste the "forbidden fruit." He wanted to come out of the closet! He informed me that he was leaving the ministry, that he would never heal and that he was going to have a great time being gay. After spewing all this venom, he then looked me in the eye and said, "And who do you think that you are kidding...you are still gay! You haven't changed either!" I paused for a second as the devil tried to convince me that what Mike was saying was true...and then from deep within, the Holy Spirit gave me the strength to proclaim the truth as the right words just gushed from my mouth... "You may not think I've healed

but I know that it's **true…and maybe you may be giving up, but I'm not!"**

Feeling very hurt and attacked by the person I had come to love as a friend and confidante really took me aback. I turned around, hastily said goodbye and ran home like a little boy that had just been assaulted by the school bully. I retreated to the old-comfortable sofa in the family room… lay down, and began to cry out to God for relief. I will never forget the pain that I felt…it was actually physical pain in my chest. I felt personally assaulted…my colleague in the fight had abandoned ranks and was leaving me alone to fight the world! He was one of our "front-runners." **Mike had all the four characteristics that had to be in place if someone is going to make it out,** he was Christian, had a conviction that the gay lifestyle was against God's desire for his life, had a desire to change and a willingness to do what it takes. The rest of us believed with certainty that he would be one of the success stories.

Many of us could empathize with the fact that he wanted to give up. What's really amazing is that many men who come to the group who are struggling with homosexuality and who have never acted upon their desires are typically jealous of the ex-gay men that have tasted the "forbidden fruit." And most of us that have been in the gay lifestyle are envious of the "virgins" because they don't have to deal with all the bad memories, of years of exposure to pornography, one-night stands and the other consequences of our carnal knowledge. Ironically, we who have been a part of the gay subculture attempt to assure the "virgins" that they aren't missing anything. As the old cliché goes, "the grass is always greener on the other side." Everybody wants what he or she doesn't have.

I knew that I could not be Mike's savior. I had to release him to God's care hoping that like me, he would soon see the errors of his ways and return to a life of holiness. After that day, I lost touch with him for quite a while until one January, five years later, while marching in the annual Pro-Life March on Washington, in the midst of a crowd of tens of thousands of people, a Franciscan monk walked up to me and yelled out, "Hey Anthony!" I looked into his eyes, not realizing who it was, and soon concluded that it was Mike.

He gave me a hug. We began to chat and he told me that he was in his last year at a Catholic seminary. He then said, "You were right. I tried it for a while, and saw the gay world for what it really is, and left it behind. God has called me out of homosexuality. Everything you told me about the gay lifestyle was true, but I had to see it for myself. Thank you for being a strong influence in my life." We embraced, shared some idle chitchat and then said our good-byes. What a wonderful gift from God to have the opportunity to run in to Mike all these years later; to know that he was walking right with the Lord.

STUART

Stuart came to the ministry in the early years. He had been raised in a typical midwestern family. He had a very distant relationship with his father and had over-bonded with his mother. He was a practicing Christian living the "double life" -- church on Sunday and the gay life on Saturday nights. God eventually asked him to choose which path he would take. He had been involved in the gay lifestyle for about four years before he started coming to TCM. He was one of the most committed members of TCM in its twelve-year history. He worked through many of the hurts of his childhood and later felt strong enough to return to Missouri where he had been raised. Then in the late nineties this young couple knocked unannounced on the front door of our house. It was Stuart and a female friend. He was in town on business and wanted Dianne and me to meet his new wife. She was lovely, inside and out.

After the four of us chatted for awhile, his wife took me aside and gave me a hug and said, "God has given me a whole man for a husband. Thank you for allowing God to use you in Stuart's healing process." They now have two children and been married for thirteen years. Stuart came to Washington DC in 1999 for the ministries 10th anniversary gala dinner and reunion. It was wonderful to see the continual healing in his life. When he came to us ten years ago, he was a bit effeminate. God had also healed that immaturity in his demeanor. To see him now as a husband, father, and a Christian leader at his local church was truly overwhelming.

LOUIS

Another great success story was a man named Louis who came to the ministry 16 years ago. He was a Washington attorney from a very prominent family, and was very influential in helping us with the initial legal formalities that had to be put in place as the ministry began to grow and prosper. He had become addicted to one-night stands, anonymous sexual encounters and was also struggling with a serious addiction to masturbation. As Louis began his personal healing process, he became interested in helping to stabilize the ministry. Of the original 20 members of the ministry, he was the one who seemed to be the most mature. The first few years of ministry were very hard, and Louis became a wonderful confidante. I'll never forget the time when, in the first year of ministry, we had about 12 members coming on a regular basis. We used to meet on Tuesday nights. That year, my birthday fell on a Tuesday. I was wavering back and forth: Should I cancel the meeting or shouldn't I? Should I be at home with my family, or, on the other hand, should I meet my obligation to be there for the members of the ministry? After much thought and prayer, I decided it best that I lead the Tuesday meeting. When I arrived at Church that night, the only person that showed up was Louis. I was quite disillusioned with the commitment of some of the members of the group. The devil was trying to get me to abandon ship, especially during that first year. When I realized that only Louis had showed up that night, I shared my frustration with him, saying, "They don't want to heal, Louis! These people are not so serious about their healing and about their walk with the Lord as you and I. I think I'm going to close the ministry down. This is too hard." Then again doubting my call I said, "And maybe God *hasn't* called me to ministry." Louis quickly reassured me and gave me a hug, saying, "Let's go out for dessert and coffee for your birthday." That evening persuaded me to keep the doors of the ministry open. What's really amazing is that this was a temptation of the devil and at the same time a test of God because the following Tuesday, *all twelve members* were in attendance! That night was one of the closest I'd ever come to giving up this work, and were it not for Louis' admonishment, I might well have shut down the ministry. I praise God that He sent him into my life at that very important time. Louis is very much responsible for the over 600 ex-gay men and women that I have ministered to since 1989. He successfully recovered from homosexuality and his related addictions and continues to be a friend and supporter of this ministry. He has been in a relationship with a woman for over six years now and my hope is that they will soon be married.

RICHARD

Probably the most extraordinary testimony that I've ever heard in my life came from a former homosexual. He had been attending a Christian AIDS ministry and came to visit our group one night and shared his story with us. I really can't take any credit for ministering to him; he attended our group only a few times, mainly for some additional encouragement and to exhort us in the first year of our ministry.

Richard came from a very dysfunctional family background. He became a homosexual prostitute and drug addict in the 1970s. By the time he came out of both addictions, he had entered a Satanic coven. By the time he left all of this behind to follow the Lord Jesus, he was a third level Satanist. I questioned him, "What does it mean to be a third level Satanist?" He told me that at that level, he was kidnapping children and digging up dead bodies for Satanic rituals. I then asked what they would do with the children and the bodies? He said during the high "holy days" of Satanic ritual, full moons and Halloween being the primary times, they would lay the freshly buried dead bodies on an "altar" to Satan. The members of the coven would then cut open the chest cavity of the dead person, pull out all the main organs and place the live baby inside the cavity. After crudely sewing it shut they would stab the baby and then offer it as a sacrifice to Satan. Afterwards, they would drink the blood of the freshly killed baby and eat the organs of the dead person as an opportunity to mock the Christian sacrament of Holy Communion. Many Satanic acts are performed to mock or be the opposite of many Christian rituals.

After taking a deep gulp, I then asked, "How did God rescue you from the heavy life that you were living?" He explained that the beginning of the end came when he went to a meeting of the Satanic coven that he was affiliated with. He mentioned that attendees at this meeting were not in what is typically thought of as "Satanic garb," rather, the meeting took place in an office setting and participants were dressed in suits and ties. It looked like any typical corporate board meeting. They informed him that they wanted to move him up to the fourth level in their coven. He was told about the benefits he would receive, including money, sex, drugs and whatever he wanted. He then asked what would be expected of him if he were moved to level four. They responded, "You would have to begin doing the Satanic rituals" – essentially the infant sacrifices! He then asked them if he could think about it overnight, and walked out of the meeting. On his way home, he walked into a park, sat down and pondered this next step in his life. He knew that he had participated in some horrible, hideous, dark crimes; however, he had never killed anyone. The remnant of what was left of his conscience began to speak to him. He felt that he could not murder. This would be crossing a serious line as far as he was concerned; so he cried out to the Lord: "God, I know that you are out there because I know whom I serve. If you could ever forgive me for what I have been doing and rescue me, I will serve you for the rest of my life." Shortly after he prayed to God, a girl about five years old, who was bouncing a ball nearby, stopped bouncing the ball and walked up to him. She looked him straight in the eye and said, "Do you know that Jesus loves you?" and then repeated, "Do you know that Jesus loves you?" and then she walked away. He just knew inside that the Lord had heard his cry for repentance and was calling him to be saved.

He was very scared, though, to leave the coven. He had actually signed his name in his own blood to Satan on a written contract. He knew that without God's protection, his fellow Satanists would kill him. *No one leaves a Satanic coven alive.* He was able to find a good Christ-centered church in suburban Maryland that specialized in spiritual warfare and deliverance ministry. They prayed for him, nurtured him, protected him, and cared for him. As he expected, the coven did come after him to kill him. But they were not successful; the Holy Spirit protected him from their retribution. He mentioned that although this happened a few years ago, the members of the coven still sought to kill him, but God's hand of protection was on him. He then began to talk about how important our testimonies were. Richard told us that he was now HIV infected and had full-flown AIDS, but that he was going to use the rest of his life to bring glory to God by warning Christians that the devil is real. He spent the rest of his life going from pulpit to pulpit warning parents about how to protect their children from demonic interference. We need to protect our children from the rise of the occult in our culture, that things like Magic Cards, Dungeons & Dragons, vampire and witchcraft television shows make our youth vulnerable to the lure of Satanism. Richard died from AIDS-related complications in the early 1990s. He preached the Good News of God's forgiveness up until the very end. He had a "holy death." The funeral was beautiful and the presence of the Holy Spirit was surely felt. I will never forget the power of Richard's testimony. Revelation 12:11-12 says, "we will overcome the devil by the blood of Jesus, **and by the word of our testimony**" because we do not love our lives unto death.

CHAPTER 12

THE CROSSES
WE MUST BEAR

T hose first few years of ministry were very exciting and, at the same time, extremely exhausting. After the ministry had established itself and had stabilized, I called Adam, the director of the ministry that Transformation had spun-off from. I felt it was time to "bury the hatchet" between the two of us. I asked him if he would come to one of our regular Tuesday night meetings and give the teaching. He accepted my invitation and presented the teaching at a meeting a few weeks later. There were about 20 men and women that were attending by that time. Afterwards Adam commented on what a wonderful ministry that God had blessed us with. He apologized for ostracizing me and the other two founders of PFM. He admitted that he had been unkind and asked my forgiveness. I then said, "We never wanted to leave the ministry that you were offering; we wanted to be a part of it! You are very much responsible for our coming out of the gay lifestyle."

We wanted to offer this "satellite" ministry in down-town Washington to help the urban gays that could not make it out to the Virginia "burbs." We wanted to honor you by helping plant seeds right in the midst of the DC gay subculture. We never wanted to split off from the ministry that you established. And then I suggested bringing TCM back under Adam's authority. He mentioned that he would prayerfully consider it and get back to me. He called a few days later and said he'd like to do that, so almost immediately we became the DC chapter of Adam's ministry. I was very excited to see the two groups working together again.

The DC group went through another growth spurt and we were seeing around thirty ex-gays on a regular basis. Everything was going quite well. For the first few years Dianne and I were financially supporting the ministry on our own. However, I began to be quite concerned that our personal savings that I'd been using to fund the ministry were beginning to dry up. At the same time my secular work income that was coming from the small architectural restoration firm I ran was being affected by the economic downturn of the early 1990s. In addition, the ministry's demands on my time increased. I didn't know what to do; my secular income was not paying the bills, so I contacted Adam and discussed my financial situation with him. I mentioned to him that I would only need about $12,000 a year to close the financial gap, and respectfully asked him to consider placing me on part-time payroll at the ministry. He told me he'd get back to me, and when he called back a few days later, he said he'd like to meet with me along with the president of the board of directors, to discuss my proposal.

Adam and Ken, the board president expressed an interest in coming out to my home to meet my wife and family. Some of the architectural projects that I had been restoring were nearby and they wanted to see examples of my work, so I invited them out to see them. After seeing some of my work projects, we walked over to my office on 11th Street to have a meeting. I was very excited about the possibility of joining the non-volunteer ministry staff and thought that the interview was just a formality– and then the unexpected happened. The board president began to ask all kinds of odd questions such as "What was that liquid in the crystal decanter on the table in the foyer of your house?" Surprised by the question, I remained calm and replied, "Ten-year old cognac we had received as a present years ago; it's been in that bottle for five years, and to be honest, the only reason it's there is that the color highlights the crystal decanter." I then asked, "Are you asking this question because you think I drink?" I mentioned that I happened to be a teetotaler but might offer a drink to a guest on a special occasion although the great majority of my friends don't drink. His questioning continued with, "I noticed a poker chip canister in one of your bedrooms. Do you gamble?" I soon began to realize where this interview was heading; however, I remained calm and responded with grace and said, "A few times a year, we have had some friends over to play poker. It was a past time where no one ever lost more than five dollars; it's was just an alternative to the movies." He then asked another ridiculous question, but this time I refused to dignify it with a response.

I became very irritated and then said, "*Is this an interview or an inquisition? Are you questioning my integrity?* If you are, all I can say is that my reputation speaks for itself. I have worked faithfully as an ex-gay minister for two and a half years. I am currently ministering to over 50% of all the attendees in your ministry and I have been faithful to my wife and healing process. All I am asking for is a small part-time salary of $12,000 so I may continue to be effective in ministering to our members."

They told me that they would not offer me a salary. They wanted me to return to full-time secular work, *and* continue to run the Tuesday night support group. I then reported that I was currently giving thirty hours a week to the ministry, and that really wasn't even enough to minister properly to the number of attendees and phone calls of inquiry. They really stunned me with their response: "Well if you lose half of them, so be it." With right displeasure, I shot back; "God has sent these thirty trusting souls to us for help. There is so little ministry out there for these very courageous ex-gays, and *every* one of them is important to Him. Even if my family has to live on food stamps, I will keep this ministry going so that we don't have to lose one single person back to the life-style." After I said this, I kicked them both out of my office.

And that's exactly what happened. We broke off from the Maryland ministry and took back the name of our old ministry, and by working all kinds of odd jobs, I was able to balance ministry and family life.

The ministry continued to flourish, and we had to move to larger quarters on 16th Street. God supplied a large meeting room that accommodated as many as fifty people. It was a very exciting time of growth for us.

At this time, we decided to host the ministry's first seminar on healing for the homosexual.

Again, I don't think we fully realized what we were getting into. The radical gay activists groups such as Queer Nation and ACT-UP who were at the height of their popularity, especially in Washington, DC were not impressed that we were hosting our First Annual Conference on *Healing for the Homosexual* near the gay section in Washington. They were even less *thrilled* that Dr. Elizabeth Moberly, the mother of the ex-gay movement, was to be its keynote speaker.

Can you picture the scene at The Carnegie Institute Building that Saturday in 1991 when the meeting was held: Over 100 conference attendees were leaving the building for a dinner break. We were walking out the front door of the building and were confronted by over 200 whistle-blowing radical gay activists with bullhorns and three-foot high posters of naked Playgirl centerfolds. They were screaming and yelling, and eventually we were forced to call the police.

Apparently the gay activists had placed a half-page adver-tisement in the Gay Blade Newspaper announcing where the conference was being held and challenged the gay commu-nity (as the campy advertisement said) *"to put on their church clothes and Sunday best and come on over to meet the attendees of this ex-gay healing conference!"*

I was never really fearful about being involved in the ex-gay movement before, but standing in the doorway of the Carnegie Institute, facing this screaming mob of angry activists, was a bit intimidating. For a second, I didn't know what to do until one of the conference attendees, a little blue-haired lady from Bethesda, MD who had a son in the life-style, walked into the midst of the demonstrators and yelled out, "What are you people doing? These people don't hate you; they are here to *help* you!" And then in a moment of "highest ex-gay drama" she pointed at the three foot-high nude male centerfold posters and screamed out, "And take down those disgusting posters of those naked people!"

Inside ourselves, we were screaming. God had used this genteel old lady to put the gay activists in their place. The gays didn't know what to do with her. God the Holy Spirit used this seemingly fragile lady to disarm their anger, and she with great authority intimidated them into silence. The whistles and horns stopped blowing; the activists were really embarrassed to be holding up their lewd signs in front of all the "church-people" that were there and quickly put them down.

What was so sophomoric about the activists was that they really thought they could intimidate us back into the gay lifestyle by tempting us with their pornographic posters *(sic)*. Under one of the signs someone had written "isn't *this* what you really want?" (referring to a good-looking poster–guy)...Just how *queeny* can you get! I really had to laugh. This gay activist "intimidation tactic" was further proof that I had made the right choice by leaving the gay lifestyle behind. Here is a group of people, who are trying to tell America that "they are all inclusive" and that people should be allowed to make their own choices about their sexuality, trying to intimidate a bunch of ex-gays to abandon their hope of having a normal life. Who here are the intolerant ones? I soon realized the fact that the ex-gay movement had become the newest minority group and the gays were discriminating against our right to exist. *Wow! What a hate crime!*

What's even more funny is that after *the blue-haired lady from Bethesda did her thing*, we were able to move into the crowd and minister to them and answer their questions, and disarm their hatred with love. It was an incredible conference and an incredible day!

The gay community was very upset by our presence in their midst; however, they were beginning to realize that **we were here, ex-queer, and that they'd have to get used to it.** Parents & Friends Ministries (PFM) was beginning to cause a lot of sparks in the gay community. They simply didn't know how to handle us. One night, the activists appeared in front of our building shortly before the meeting with an eight-foot high cross, on which they hung a gay activist in a gold lame' loincloth. They tried to intimidate our ministry members from coming into the building that night, but they were not successful.

As the meeting began, six lesbians with severe haircuts walked into the meeting and sat down. My assistant kept kicking me under the table and whispering to me, "What are you going to do about this?" My first instinct was to call the police and have them evicted from the building, but then an inner voice spoke very clearly and said, "These women have been rejected all their lives, just allow them to stay and show them how helpful this ministry is." That night, an ex-gay gave his one-year testimony talking about how this ministry had impacted his life. We then watched a video-tape of an appearance that I had recently done on a television talk show. The lesbians were silent during the entire meeting; and at the end, one raised her hand and asked to speak. "Sure," I replied, "We sort of figured who you guys are." "We came here to find out what Transformation was all about," one of the lesbian activists replied. "Although we do not believe that homosexuality is wrong, we see that you do not hate gay people, and we're actually surprisingly impressed by this group and realize that you serve a purpose for people who are unhappy being gay." I told them that the political gay community was telling them a lot of lies about who we really are, and that I was glad that they came to see for themselves. We hugged each other, and then they left the meeting. After that, the gay activists began to back off and have hardly bothered us since.

CHAPTER 13

SEIZING THE MOMENT:
ENTERING THE MEDIA
SPOTLIGHT

The numbers began to grow, the group began to mature spiritually, and we began to add small group leaders. The ministry began to flourish, we were able to hire a small full-time staff and now it was time for me to begin to promote the ex-gay movement on a national and international scale. **It was time to spread the Good News to the gay community that there was freedom from homosexuality through the name of Jesus Christ**! Although the media were generally hostile to our cause, they were curious and began to call us more and more for interviews. I probably have done over 150 interviews in the last 15 years. This would include everything from television to newspaper and countless amounts of radio interviews. I soon realized that God was calling me to be a media spokesman for the ex-gay movement and I really enjoyed doing it. My testimony was unusual, true and interesting to the media (Christian and secular) and after being a part of the gay community for almost a decade, I could speak with authority about what really goes on in the gay subculture. While I had never had any formal media training, practice does make perfect, and I became more media savvy the more interviews I did. I am utterly amazed by the sheer power and impact the media has had on our culture. It clearly is the vehicle to use to reach the masses with the ex-gay message. Unfortunately the gay political lobbyists have figured this out. Just when you think that you wasted your time by appearing on a TV or radio show with a liberal host, you'd be amazed to see how God will work even in the midst of an interview that you think was not effective.

My first media appearance was a radio interview. I'll never forget it! The word "ex-gay" was a relatively new phenomenon on the Washington scene in 1990. It was a live broadcast that aired from the very liberal, American University. It was called *The Fred Fisk Show*, which could be heard in the greater Washington, DC metro area.

I hadn't realized that interviewers could be such vipers! This interviewer was obviously hostile to my presence on his show and clearly had a pre-planned agenda to try to discredit me. I was really on the defensive and really felt beat-up by the time that very *long* hour had passed. Not realizing that the Lord was with me all the time, I left the radio station feeling spiritually beat-up. After a cold "thank-you-for- being-on-the-show" from Mr. Fisk I walked out of the studio with my head hung low.

After I jumped into my car and knew that was alone I cried out to God, "Why did you put me through that? What was your purpose?" My question was soon answered that following Monday morning when the phone in my office rang. The caller on the other end identified himself as Don, and told me that he had heard me on the radio, and that he, too, was an ex-gay. He then mentioned that he'd come out of homosexuality without any help or support. He also mentioned he was financially successful and was interested in helping the ministry flourish. He asked what we needed for our office.

We had just opened our first office on 11ᵗʰ St. because I couldn't continue to operate the administration of the ministry out of a small office in our home. Our daughter was getting older and we needed to start being discreet with our telephone conversations. You can only imagine some of the topics of discussion some of our phone calls included.

We didn't have many assets back then, and I informed Ron that we needed the basics such as a desk, a chair, a telephone and an answering machine. He then asked what we *really* needed, and I boldly replied that we needed a copy machine. He said, "No, you don't understand. I'm rich. What do you *really* need?" I then became very bold and replied, "OK, we need a computer system!" A few weeks later, an $8,000 computer system was delivered to my office. I was very humbled. God was beginning to supply the material needs that were necessary to accomplish the task He had set before us.

The word had to get out that there was freedom from homosexuality through Jesus Christ. I have always been a very bold person, not having any problem communicating, even on difficult or awkward subjects. No one could ever accuse me of being shy or demure. When the Lord saves us, He doesn't give us a brand-new personality; He will usually use the persona that He gave us and clean up anything that is not of Him. My biggest fear when I became a Christian was that I would now have to be quiet and wear polyester leisure suits. The Lord showed me that I didn't have to do either (thank God!). He used my bold, New York Italian-Jewish personality to come up against the rhetoric of the radical pro-gay political activists and the talk-speak of the revisionist media. The Lord does not give us a spirit of timidity, as 2 Timothy 1:7 says, but rather a spirit of boldness to proclaim the Good News.

In the early 1990s, there were very few ex-gay media spokesmen other than Sy Rogers confronting the media lies and propaganda head-on concerning gay issues. I loved doing it; I had no idea what I was opening myself up to spiritually, but truly enjoyed "stepping up to the plate" as an ex-gay apologist.

THE JANE WHITNEY SHOW

The first national television show that I did was the Jane Whitney Show, out of Boston. The theme of the show was should homosexuality be taught to high school students as an alternative lifestyle? This media "exercise" really "baptized" me into the seriousness of the "politically correct" agenda that was beginning to permeate America.

The scenario with most talk shows is basically the same; they call you on the phone, flatter you, tell you how important you are to the show, fly you up, limousine at the airport, wine and dine you, fatten you up, and then throw you to the lions. Representing the Christian point of view were I, a woman named Edie Gieb who was fighting the gay agenda in the California public school system, and a high school student. The show's strategy was "keep all the Christians separated and non-unified." Put the pro-gay contingent on during the first few taped segments, load up the audience with gays and their sympathizers. After winning the audience over, drag the Christians into the arena, and let the slaughter begin.

That was what the producer of this show intended. However the Lord had his way, and used Edie, the young Christian student, and me for His glory. After they did our makeup and "miked" us, we were escorted into a dressing room and given a "pep talk" by a large, hulking female producer. She informed us that we would not come on until the end of the show. When she noticed that Edie and the student were holding a Bible and some pro-gay children's books, the producer informed us that we could not bring them on national TV. She further informed us that the "Heather Has Two Mommies" and "Daddy's Roommate" books were a no-no; further, there would be no TV monitor in our dressing room – which meant we wouldn't know what was being discussed by the panel prior to our appearance on stage. Basically, we were being set up for an ambush.

My blood began to boil. Righteous indignation welled up within me and I replied that that was not acceptable. I then stated, "There should be no reason why we can't bring our Bibles on national TV, and the 'gay children's books' are necessary to show America exactly the kind of propaganda these gay advocates are imposing on our children. I didn't fly out from Washington DC and take two days away from the office, nor did Edie and her student friend fly from the West Coast, to appear on the last 15 minutes of a talk show." She replied, "Tough. Take it or leave it." I turned to Edie and the student and said, "Are you ready to walk, because I am." They looked at me, smiled, and said, "Yes, let's get out of here." I turned to the producer and said, "You don't have a show." She quickly positioned herself in front of the dressing room door, blocking our exit, and said; "You ain't goin' nowhere." I answered, "If you don't move yourself from that door in the next three seconds, you'll have our staff of attorneys in here to answer to." In a split-second, her whole demeanor changed; she then said, "What do you want?"

We negotiated for a few minutes, and the final outcome was that we were able to come on in the first few segments, and we'd have a monitor in our dressing room. But she was so intimidated by the Bible and the pro-gay children's propaganda books that she would not allow them on. We accepted her terms, and the show taping was very successful. When it finally aired, the show was balanced, the Christians weren't butchered, and we were able to present a Christ-centered warning to America about the political gay agenda's plans for propagandizing our children.

The gay politicos know perfectly well that most of the "over 45" America will never fall for their propaganda that the gay lifestyle is *just* an alternative lifestyle. They know that if they are going to persuade America to vote for gay "marriage" and gay "civil rights" that they will have to persuade the minds of young Americans. And let me tell you, they are doing a great job! If America doesn't slap this spoiled child called "the gay political movement" on the rump soon...all will be lost.

THE RICKI LAKE SHOW

When I had the opportunity to appear on the first televised Ricki Lake Show, it felt odd arriving at the studio that day. Everybody who worked there was dressed in black; it was a very "New Age" group. Perhaps because of this, but perhaps also for some other unknown reason, I was nervous about appearing on this show. I also knew that Ricki was one of the "darlings" of the gay community. Years ago when I was a homosexual, I remember her appearing in the movie "Hairspray" with the famous drag queen, Divine. I knew what I was getting myself into when I accepted the invitation.

After being greeted by the producer, I was escorted onto the set and directed to "makeup." As the cosmetician was applying my makeup, she asked the question, "What are you on the show for today?" I took a deep breath, thinking quickly before I answered: makeup artist, New York City, Ricki Lake Show. If I tell her what I'm here for, she'll probably deliberately botch my makeup and I'll end up with large black circles under my eyes on national TV! However I felt the Holy Spirit say, "Just tell her what you do." So I answered, "I'm an ex-gay. I came out of the lifestyle a number of years ago and I have a ministry in Washington DC to recovering homosexuals."

She looked surprised, and I expected a hostile, "politically correct" response. Instead, she asked me if I minded if she shut the door to the dressing room. She did so, and exclaimed, "You're an ex-gay? I'm a Christian, and I volunteer for the local ex-gay ministry in New York City!" I said, "Are you kidding?" She said, "No. It's pretty dark working here, but it's a mission field. Let's pray before you go on the air." It was just what the doctor ordered; it relaxed me, and I was able to come up against seven pro-gay panelists and successfully deflected all of their "PC" arguments. The studio audience eventually sided with me, and the show triggered many calls to Exodus International for help.

THE GERALDO SHOW

Most of the talk shows that I have participated in have had "loaded" panels, stacked with those opposed to the ex-gay movement and/or Christianity in general. The Geraldo Show was no exception, and its panel was one of the more interesting ones of which I've been a part.

This time I appeared with one of the founders of the ex-gay movement, Dr. Charles Socarides, the famous New York psychiatrist who worked with ex-gays in the 1950s, and also with an ex-lesbian named Jane Boyer. We were called to oppose several militant gay activists. Geraldo was obviously taking their side and not giving us enough time to speak. I recall that one of the psychiatrists, Dr. Robert Spitzer, who was "responsible" for lobbying the APA (the American Psychiatric Association) to remove homosexuality from the DSM-III (the APA's official digest of mental illnesses) in 1974, was also on the panel. He *bragged* about his pivotal role in the DSM-III change. I couldn't believe that he was boasting about it. I had had no plans to say it, but a righteous indignation boiled up from within and I said, "Dr. Spitzer, because of what you did in 1974, you affirmed a whole generation of young men and women into the gay lifestyle.

Now, many of these men are dying, or are already dead, from AIDS. I don't think that's anything to brag about." He was silent, unable to respond, and said little during the rest of the program.

One exchange that I fondly remember was the following one: Geraldo said to me, "So what if you'd had many male sexual partners. What's wrong with that? I'm hetero-sexual, and I've had many female partners." My response was, "Geraldo, we can get help for you too." Wouldn't you know, that little part of the taping was cut from the show and never aired? I was beginning to realize that even if you were successful in communicating intelligent warnings about what the gay political agenda was truly about, you weren't even guaranteed they would air it!

THE SALLY JESSE RAPHAEL SHOW

I am often criticized for doing the talk show circuit. Even some of my peers have judged me and have made statements claiming that appearances on the talk shows are a waste of time. I disagree. Jesus always went where the sinners were. He did not come to save those who are already walking in righteousness; He came to save the lost, the sick, and the ones who know they need a Savior. As the New Testament vividly communicates, Jesus went *to look* for the sinners. He broke bread with tax collectors' and talked to prostitutes, adulterers, etc., much to the chagrin of the Pharisees and Seduces. They found these actions scandalous; however, that did not stop the Lord from doing His Father's will.

You won't find many practicing homosexuals in church on Sunday in the type of church where the "love the sinner, hate the sin" message is being preached. However, many gays watch the talk shows and it's an incredible mission field! When negotiating with the producers of The Sally Show, I felt the Holy Spirit urging me to insist on having the phone number for Parents & Friends Ministries appear on-screen during the credits, and they agreed.

This by far was one of the toughest shows I'd ever appeared on however; it turned out to be one of the most successful. It was I, alone, against seven lesbian activists, most of whom had left their husbands – and sometimes children – to enter the lifestyle. The studio audience was also stacked against me. One lesbian activist, accompanied on the panel by her pre-teen child, bragged about how wonderful her new life was. She then complained about the discrimination her child was suffering because her daughter's fellow students at school were teasing her about "having two mommies." The poor child was in tears, trying to defend her mother's adulterous and unnatural actions. My heart broke for the little girl. After the lesbian activist made her statement about her lifestyle choices, I asked her how she could further humiliate her daughter by bringing her on national TV to talk about her lesbianism, and then asked her, "What kind of mother are you?" The audience bellowed their approval of my statements and erupted in applause. Surprisingly, I began to win them over. When the lesbian activists realized that I was beginning to woo the audience, they turned on me and trying to discredit me. They were successfully justifying their lifestyle choices until a young Christian lady in the audience stood up and eloquently blasted them saying, "It was OK for you to go from **straight to gay** by divorcing your husbands. Why wouldn't it be possible for him to go from being **gay to being straight**?" The audience went wild. The Lord used her simple statement to clearly communicate the truth of the ex-gay message of hope, and we earned the support of the studio audience from that point on.

The epilogue to this story is remarkable. The show aired approximately three weeks later, and we brought in extra staff to handle the anticipated flood of calls. Around 10:00 AM, one of the phone counselors took a call from a young man in southern Virginia who informed us that he had just taken 32 valiums three hours before. He was lying in front of the TV set, dying, when he saw me on TV. As the credits rolled, he read our telephone number and was able to get to a phone to call us, and said, "I saw that ex-gay man on TV. My father raped me when I was ten; I've been gay for many years; I've never been happy being gay and never knew that I could get out of it... I want to live! Please help me." We were able to find out what town he lived in and called the local police. They contacted an ambulance squad, broke into his apartment, and rescued him. A life was saved that day, and it was then that I understood why the Holy Spirit urged me to request our phone number be displayed during the credits on the Sally show.

PAT ROBERTSON, THE 700 CLUB

When this invitation came to appear on The 700 Club, I was very excited. What a great opportunity to minister to the Christian community about what God was doing in the midst of the repentant homosexual community! This was the first opportunity that I had to appear on a national Christian television show. What a wonderful thought that I would be interviewed by Terry Meeuwsen, Pat Robertson's co-host; finally, a user-friendly interviewer!

I drove to Virginia Beach, VA from Washington, DC the night before, but left my suit at home! I couldn't believe it. What was I going to do? Luckily, the staffer who greeted me when I arrived at the Founder's Inn was about my size. I explained my dilemma, and he offered to lend me a suit. This employee seemed, a bit nervous around me, and I couldn't discern why; however, he soon "spilled the beans" and confessed his own struggle with homosexuality. I was able to minister to him that night and continued afterwards to minister to him.

One of the bellhops at the hotel approached me and said, "I recognized you and know who you are. I am also struggling with homosexuality. Thank God you're here to bring the message to Pat Robertson and the staff of The 700 Club that God can heal the homosexual. That message needs to be preached here." It was really remarkable: wherever I turned during those two days at the 700 Club compound, the Lord used me to minister to someone who was either gay and struggling, or who had a friend or family member who was gay.

As I was checking into the Founder's Inn, there was a line at the reception desk. I began to talk to a man standing next to me. After opening pleasantries, he asked what I was there for. I hesitated a moment before telling him and then said that I was an ex-gay who was to appear on The 700 Club the next morning. He exclaimed, 'you're an ex-gay? I am a convert to Christianity from Judaism, and I'm here for the Messianic Jewish Conference. I'm here to give my testimony at the conference about that. My pastor loves it when I give testimony about my conversion to Christianity; however, when I've told him that God has also brought me out of homosexuality, he has always instructed me to leave *that* part out of my testimony. He then said, "I have always felt that I should give the *full* story of what God has done in my life, and that I should not be ashamed of the way God has transformed my sexuality." I exhorted him to add the story of the restoration of his heterosexuality to his testimony, so that it would be complete. He thanked me; we hugged, and went our ways.

I woke up the next morning, stuffed my borrowed suit so that it would fit better, and went down to the TV studio for the live broadcast. I must admit that doing The 700 Club was a bit intimidating. I was upset that Mr. Robertson was not doing the interview personally, but really enjoyed being interviewed by Terry Meeuwsen. She was kind and asked wonderful questions.

Pat sat off-camera and listened attentively to the entire interview. What was really funny was when Terry asked the question, "Is it true that you were very promiscuous when you were a homosexual?" And when I answered, "Yes, I had over 400 sexual partners," Pat Robertson *gasped loudly.* So loudly, in fact, that it is audible on the videotaped copy of the interview. At the end of the interview as we went to a commercial, Mr. Robertson walked up to me, shook my hand, and said, "You have changed my entire understanding of homosexuals. Thank you."

The following week, Pat Robertson announced on his show, "Do you remember the former homosexual who appeared on my show last week? The Lord has had me up in the middle of the night, praying for him and his ministry."

Pat Robertson later sent a $10,000 check to the ministry when he found out how badly underfunded we were. Up to that time, it was the largest gift we'd ever received towards our work. I was extremely humbled to realize that the Lord had used me, a former prostitute homosexual sex addict, to change the heart of one of today's greatest evangelical leaders. We received over 100 letters and gifts of support. This one speaking engagement was a turning point for the ministry; the fruits of being faithful to the Lord included more invitations to speak, long-term donors, and many kind words of encouragement. I thank-God for the work of The 700 Club. Pat Robertson was one of the first major Christian leaders to fully support the ex-gay movement.

THE ROSEANNE SHOW

This was, by far, the most interesting national secular interview I've ever done. Knowing Roseanne Barr's former reputation, I was really expecting to have my head cut off and handed to me on a platter. What I didn't realize was that at the time of my interview, Roseanne was beginning to return to her conservative Jewish roots. I flew into Los Angeles and had the opportunity to have Charlton Heston's (a.k.a. Moses) chauffeur for a few days. It was very interesting to learn what a genuinely down-to-earth Christian that Charlton Heston really was. It was so sad to receive the news that Mr. Heston has died. He was a true Christian presence in the darkness of Hollywood.

This was my first time in Los Angeles since I had left homosexuality behind. It felt peculiar returning there. I couldn't believe how much more spiritually dark this oasis of warm sunshine and palm trees had become. The day before the interview, I had some free time, so my driver took me shopping on Rodeo Drive. I walked into an elegant designer boutique to find a gift for my wife. Out of curiosity, I looked at the tag on an evening gown that I thought she would like, and was shocked to see a $16,000 price tag. The very attentive salesman rushed over and asked if he could be of any assistance. He said, "Don't you just love it! And it's 50% off." I remarked, "Oh, that's *great*." I walked out of the store wondering, "do these people in Hollywood have a clue of how the rest of America lives?" Now I could understand more fully how these strange movies are being produced in Hollywood. I believe most people in this Hollywood/Rodeo Drive subculture are not in touch with the rest of the world.

The next morning, I woke up, ready for the interview. The driver picked me up to take me to the studio. Just before the taping began, I was introduced to Roseanne. She welcomed me, and we chatted for a while. Surprisingly, she was genuinely kind and interested in my work. Knowing from my research that she was a survivor of incest, I mentioned that I also was an over-comer in that area of my life. She looked me straight in the eye, and we clicked.

From then on something told me that this was going to be a great interview. In her opening monologue she let the viewing audience know that the show's topic today was on whether people could be healed from homosexuality. She then said to the audience that they might be quite surprised to hear her stand on this subject, and then on air she mentioned that she had lost a brother to AIDS. Therefore, I wasn't surprised to realize that some of her responses were cautiously supportive.

When the studio audience (which the producer had loaded with gay activists) began to challenge me, Roseanne actually defended me. The actress Sharon Stone was sitting in the audience and attacked me verbally, and Roseanne came to my rescue again. What was also amazing about this taping was that the producer had invited about twenty ex-gays to be a part of the studio audience. During the taping they prayed and were also a very productive part of the debate when Roseanne opened up the panel to questions from the studio audience. We really won this one. It was a great victory for the ex-gay movement. This was the first time that I know of when a secular national talk show host favored our side and where the studio audience was balanced.

The epilogue to this story is that some of the board members from the Human Rights Campaign Fund (which is the country's largest gay political lobbying group) were sitting in the studio audience. After the taping, the guests from the show were in the green room having lunch, and we were all sitting at the same table. When I found out who they were, I invited them to have dinner later that evening and, surprisingly, they accepted. I was able to minister to them that evening before my plane left.

FOCUS ON THE FAMILY, RADIO SHOW

I had often heard of Dr. James Dobson and his ministry, and I understand that his show is one of the most listened-to Christian radio shows in the United States. I was honored when Bob Knight, Director of Cultural Affairs at the Family

Research Council (FRC) in Washington, DC, arranged an interview for the two of us on Dobson's radio show. Soon thereafter I received a phone call from one of Focus' producers extending the invitation for me to join Bob Knight on the show. I asked him if we could conduct the interview by telephone because it would involve flying out to Colorado, which meant two days away from the office and that we were shorthanded. He mentioned that Dobson preferred to have his guests "in-studio," so I agreed to fly out. Before I hung up I asked the producer if their travel agent would call me to make flight arrangements. His response shocked me: "No, I don't think you understand. You're going to have to pay your own way out here." Typical protocol when one is invited to be a guest on a TV or radio show is that the show is responsible for transportation, lodging and guests' meals. I thought it odd that they insisted that I be in-studio *and* expected our struggling ministry to be responsible for the traveling expenses. After getting off the phone with the producer, I telephoned Bob Knight over at FRC to get some advice and make sure that I wasn't overreacting. Bob seemed a bit surprised that Focus was unwilling to take care of my travel arrangements. At the time, our annual budget was about $90,000, compared to Focus' budget of about $115 million. I couldn't believe it. Bob, being a devoted supporter of the ex-gay movement, arranged airline tickets somehow, and in late January 1997, I flew to Colorado Springs for the taping of the show.

The morning of the interview, I arrived at the Focus on the Family compound. It was immense and quite impressive. After passing through security, I was escorted into Dr. Dobson's imposing office to meet with him before the taping began. He seemed to be a very nice, cordial man. After some casual conversation, I asked Dr. Dobson if he would consider taping two or three shows. I mentioned that since Bob Knight and I had come all the way out from Washington,

DC and would be in Colorado for a couple of days away from the office, it would be good use of time. I suggested that the interviews could be kept "in a can" and air at a later date. I was taken aback when he responded "**Anthony, to be honest with you, most of our listeners will find this subject pretty distasteful and probably couldn't take more than one show on this subject.**' I couldn't believe that he would say such a thing. I don't think he realized how many Christian families were suffering with this issue and how powerful the political gay community was getting. I believe that his response was highly insensitive.

I then asked him if he could air the broadcast sometime in February because we were having our annual Parents & Friends Christian Ministries National Conference in early March and could use some promotion of the conference. Again I was very disappointed to hear him say that this was impossible, and that it wouldn't air until April or May because of production schedules and red tape. I was very disappointed at the thought of this missed opportunity to let parents know about the conference, but didn't press it even though I really felt an "inner voice" telling me at least to ask him.

I think he was quite naïve as to how many persons were out there struggling with this issue. If statistics are correct that approximately 3% of the population is gay, then that means there are over 8 million homosexuals in the U.S; and equally important, it also means there are probably at least 30 million people who are also affected – parents, siblings, friends – by the issue of homosexuality. He also seemed unaware that homosexuality affects not only those struggling with it but also those close to them. It seems that Dr. Dobson was very interested in fighting the gay political agenda, which is admirable, but not mindful of the great part of his listening audience that homosexuality touches.

We taped before a live studio audience, and Jim Dobson could not stop asking questions. What was scheduled to be a half-hour interview extended to two hours. I believe God used Bob and me to enlighten this Christian leader on how much He loves the homosexual person and on how much ground the gay political movement has gained. The interview also touched on the prospect of gay marriage, a referendum issue then before the voters in Hawaii. And from that, God answered my request for additional days during which the subject would be presented on his show; because right after we finished the taping, Dobson called in one of his producers and said, "This is very timely information. How quickly can we get this on?" The producer looked at her clipboard and said, "Dr. Dobson, by coincidence we have three 'dead days' next week." He asked if they could get the interview edited in time, and she answered, "Yes." I couldn't believe what was unfolding before my eyes. The Lord wanted more time granted for this interview, and He wanted it aired in time for the Parents & Friends Conference. The program was also used by God to warn Christians in Hawaii about the gay lobbyists' push for gay "marriage" in their state. As the Bible says, "we can make whatever plans we want, but the Lord will determine our paths". Amazingly over 300 persons attended the conference, *and* "gay marriage" was voted down in Hawaii.

What was really the most tragic let-down about the Focus on the Family interview was that shortly after we finished taping the show on *ministry to homosexuals*, one of the producers walked up to me, congratulated me on how well the interview went, and then said, "Anthony, I overheard that you and your wife have had to live on food stamps to keep your ministry going. It's unforgivable that the ex-gay movement can't get the funding it needs to do this important work; Focus on the Family should be helping you. He apologized for Focus' callousness and oversight. He gave me a hug and thanked me for coming.

The reality is that homosexuality **does** touch "good Christian families" because when the radio program aired in mid-February, Focus on the Family received over 4,000 phone calls of inquiry. We were able to receive some of the overflow phone calls that Focus received in response to the three-day broadcast of the interview. Parents from all over the country began to realize that the Lord had heard their prayers and that Parents & Friends Ministries was there to equip them.

WASHINGTON CITY PAPER

In 1999 the City Paper, which reported the first major story about my work with the ministry (ten years earlier), decided to look at the issue again and called us to arrange an interview. I was a bit uneasy about trusting them again after the way that they had treated Kate Boo when she had done a very well-balanced report on our movement. With much trepidation, I contacted the reporter and accepted their request to write a story.

A free-lance reporter for the City Paper named Patrick Tracey came to cover the ministry. It was a major story. He followed us around for three days. He came to one of our support meetings. He hung out at the office just to see what a typical day at the office was like, and he also interviewed some of the ex-gay members of the ministry. The most interesting event that he accompanied me to was a pro-gay "religious" conference at Foundry United Methodist Church. Foundry is located in downtown Washington and is where former-President & Mrs. Clinton attended Sunday services. Could you believe that the church where the President of the United States attends was having a pro-gay conference? There were many of the "gay religious" present pushing a feigned religious agenda down the throats of over 400 non-suspecting attendees. Many of the "ministers" and the literature that they promoted took Holy Scripture and distorted its meaning with*revisionist apostate theology.* There was a lot of political propaganda flying around that sanctuary that day. And when a lesbian activist, who is a professor at a New Jersey college began to speak from the main pulpit at the President's church and began to tell the conference attendees that the gay movement needs to begin to align itself with other *religious* organizations such as the Wicca Society (an organization of gay and straight people that practice witch-craft), no one objected, not even President Clinton's pastor, whom I saw sitting in the second pew. I couldn't stand it anymore. Immediately following her presentation, I stood and asked her, "Are you *telling* us that the gay community needs to align itself with witchcraft?"

The reality that a woman who has left her marriage, husband and children to pursue a lesbian relationship and recommended that the gay community align itself with witch-craft was allowed to speak from the pulpit of the President's church is stunning. This was a sad day for America and is only an example of where this country is headed if we do not return to honoring the God that we formerly trusted in. It is scandalous that the pastor, who is the President's spiritual advisor, did not object to her credentials nor, when he had the opportunity to do so, did he object to the content of her presentation! This is the same minister who announced to America that he would be one of the three ministers who would hold President Clinton accountable for his sexual infidelities! It's amazing to see how little flack Sen. Barack Obama received over his pastor's leftist non-Christian views and how Hillary Clinton isn't held to any accountability for her membership in the liberal biblically-apostate church where she is a member. After questioning the speaker's credibility publicly during the Q&A session I was immediately escorted out of the Foundry Methodist Church sanctuary by two ushers. Patrick, the reporter, was incensed that I was not allowed to make politically *incorrect* public statements without facing expulsion. To no one's surprise, when the front-page article was finally published weeks later; the incident at the President's church was left out; and although the reporter was rather fair with his observations of the ministry; one could tell that someone did a final edit and botched the article.

POLITICALLY INCORRECT

I had declined an invitation to be a guest on Politically Incorrect with Bill Maher in the late 1990's because of its leftist leanings. However, I decided to accept a later invitation to appear when a new movie parodying the ex-gay movement was released in the summer of 2000. The movie was really B-quality trash and filled with misrepresentations of the ex-gay movement; however, it provided a unique opportunity to promote the work of Parents & Friends Ministries (PFM). At first they wanted to put three gay activists up against me. I knew that along with Bill Maher's pro-gay leanings that the deck would be unevenly stacked against me, so I negotiated with them until they finally agreed to allow an ex-lesbian friend come on with me. It would now be two against two; and after working out all the details, Lynne Harding and I flew to Los Angeles for the taping.

Lynne had no-fear facing the media with what God had done in her life. I also wanted to give her some additional media experience because she really was quite a natural but needed some polish. The Holy Spirit had done quite a bit of healing in her life on the inside. However, after being in the lifestyle for many years she was still a little "rough around the edges." So we spent two days in Hollywood "doing her over." We went to the most glamorous salons and shops in West Hollywood and on Rodeo Drive having her hair coiffed, her nails done, and selecting the perfect outfit for her. We went to the beach so that she could work on her tan. The make-up girl at CBS Studios helped, and by the time we walked onto the set Lynne looked fantastic.

We debated the campy Ru Paul Charles and the producer of the B-movie and with God's help we held our own. Lynne did quite well and millions of people who had never heard about the ex-gay movement heard about our ministry that night.

Many people often ask me, "Why do you even bother to go on those shows? They always attack you!" My answer usually is, "If Jesus were walking this earth today, I don't think that he would have any problem accepting an invitation to be on a liberal TV show. He always went where the action was. He loved to preach in the public square. He always went where He could find the lost, and what better place to "drop your net" than on the late-night talk-show circuit!

CHAPTER 14

THE RUBBER HITS THE ROAD

⁂

As the ministry continued to mature, we noticed that a few members needed more than lay spiritual-counsel. They also needed a place to live. Constantine was a former homosexual prostitute who had been living on the streets. Patty was an ex-lesbian single mom who needed housing for herself and her daughter. Bill was from the Richmond, Virginia area and wanted to leave the gay lifestyle behind, but didn't have two nickels to rub together. I didn't know what to do in these situations, but I did know that at the time, that there were only two ministries in the U.S. with ex-gay live-in programs.

Rather than going to the Lord in prayer and asking Him for guidance in handling these situations, I reacted, unfortunately, more to the immediate, pressing needs that existed. Without taking the time to research properly the commitment of opening an ex-gay live-in program, I went ahead and rented a house in the Logan Circle area of Washington DC, the same neighborhood in which my family and I lived.

When I came out of homosexuality, I was excited just to know that a support group existed. My reverence for the

Lord gave me a genuine, heartfelt gratitude for the healing that was available to me. Although the group I attended for my healing was relatively small, my gratitude towards them led me to do anything I could to help strengthen the group. However, when I opened the live-in program, I was dismayed to find that some of the participants in our program lacked the fear of the Lord. I couldn't believe that many of the new members of the live-in program were not taking their healing seriously.

Scripture says in Proverbs 1, "The fear of the Lord is the beginning of all wisdom and knowledge." Many of the live-in members lacked this regard for the Lord and appreciated the grace He had extended to them. There was also a great disregard for the leadership of the ministry: the small group leaders, the house director, and me. Some examples that come to mind are shocking and hard to believe, but are true. There was Bill, who struggled with a slight chemical addiction in addition to homosexuality. He had the nerve in a time of temptation one night to have drugs delivered to the live-in house. When I found out about this, I took Bill aside and asked him to try to imagine what would happen if that drug dealer knew that this was a Christian recovery house, blurted this out publicly and tried to harm the ministry's reputation – and the name of Christ. Good thing for all parties: the drug-dealer ripped-off Bill and never delivered the goods!

Another "problem" person was Harry, a former cross-dresser. Other than this 'unique eccentricity' he appeared normal. Wrong! One evening we received a phone call from him because he had been arrested at Lord & Taylor Department Store for stealing a pair of earrings. When I was in the gay subculture I can tell you that I had been around the block and wasn't a naive boy from Kansas; however, when Harry came home that night after he had been released from jail and told me his whole story. I was astounded. Harry also was a drag queen and performed in shows for pay. He apparently had stolen all of the costumes used in his former life, literally tens of thousands of dollars worth of evening gowns, shoes, makeup, lingerie, and wigs – everything. He gave me many accounts of how he would walk into the finest department stores in any part of the country and boldly unzip the evening gowns on the mannequin, drop them into a shopping bag, (because clothing on mannequins doesn't usually have security tags), and then nonchalantly walk out of the store.

And then there was Warren, who came in after house curfew one night. Leadership was ready to lambaste him for his continual disregard for the house rules, but before we could, he broke out in tears telling us a terrible story of how he had been raped by his former boyfriend that night. We felt terribly guilty for chastising him and decided we should take him to the hospital to be examined. It was about midnight when we drove him to the local hospital accompanied by all the live-in members, and waited in the emergency room for over three hours while he was examined.

Police were called in to take the report, and we prayed for him while we waited. After several hours, the attending doctor and police officer came to inform us that Warren was lying. They went on to say that they had examined him from head to toe and found *no* evidence whatsoever that he'd been harmed in any way! They first recommended that he be arrested for filing a false police report but then relented and told us to get him out of there. As you probably have guessed by now, Warren was a pathological liar and had made up the entire story to cover up his lateness. We eventually had to ask him to leave the program because of his unwillingness to work his program.

Just when you have begun to think that these stories are outrageous, along comes Todd. He was a former male prostitute who worked Capitol Hill. He worked for a high-class callboy service whose clients included members of Congress and high-level government staff, and wanted out.

He wanted desperately to be accepted into the program and needed to "disappear" because of the threat to his safety posed by leaving the prostitution service knowing what he knew. The night that he informed the management of the callboy service that he was leaving, they decided to rough him up just in case he decided to tell anyone about some of the famous names in Washington government that they "serviced."

He really had us concerned that the Mafia might retaliate against him or us. Fortunately this one time beating was the last retribution that Todd experienced from them. It certainly was a bit scary taking him in to the live-in program, but we had to give him the benefit of doubt to see if he was really serious about change. Todd was raised by a Christian mother and knew about Jesus, but unfortunately, was blinded by money and the high life and eventually did return to the lifestyle. Amazingly just last year, Todd found the ministry website and phone number and called me at 3 o'clock in the morning to inform me that he had finally left the gay lifestyle behind and had been clean for over two years.

One night, one of the members of the live-in house walked into the bathroom and caught nineteen-year-old Sammy from Florida burning an upside down crucifix in the sink. We were all floored to learn that a program member had the audacity to do Satanic rituals in a Christian recovery house. We had to ask Sam to leave the house. His was too much of a negative influence on the rest of the men. The straw that broke the camel's back happened one night when the leadership and house members had just returned after a social outing. When we turned on the lights in the front parlor of the large antique townhouse that we occupied, our eyes were immediately drawn to the beautifully carved marble fireplace. Carved into the center of the ornate mantle was an angel, but what was really odd was that its eyes had been burned out and darkened, apparently with a cigarette lighter. We all stared at the carving, completely taken aback for a moment. Then almost in unison we yelled, "Sam! It had to be Sammy!" We were furious! This magnificent town-house had survived relatively unscathed, one hundred and forty years of history in our nation's Capital – including the riots of the 1960s and the Great Depression – until Sammy. If we hadn't asked him to leave, I believe he would eventually have burned the house down. If the angel did not clean up before the landlord came over for his next visit, we would have a lot of explaining to do. Part of Sam's penance was to scrub the angel clean. Thank God it cleaned up well enough so that the landlord didn't notice.

Bill from Montana was another memorable live-in program resident – and not for good reason: He had the most wonderful parents. His father was a farmer who worked hard but was an absentee dad. His mother was dominant in his upbringing and really did not allow him to grow-up. They were ready and willing to take responsibility for their short-comings and were not in denial.

They were not wealthy people but were able to provide all the program expenses for him to work on his homosexual issues. They even accompanied him on his initial trip to DC to meet the staff and make sure that he was in a safe environment before returning to their farm. We had some wonderful sessions together where Bill's parents tearfully shared with him the problems in their marriage and his father's lack of attention to him due to work demands. Bill's heartfelt response was touching; some real healing was occurring in him, and he showed great potential. No sooner had his parents left, however, than his whole demeanor changed, practically overnight. "Young gay farm boy hits city," and without his parents, he decided to make life a living hell for the leadership.

What he didn't realize was that we knew the boundaries he needed, and that if he did not comply, then he'd be put out of the house. To show the depth of his rebellion and arrogance, one day while we were all at our regular jobs, Bill defiled the house by bringing a man, whom he'd picked up on the street, to the house for a sexual interlude. When I found out that he'd done this, I couldn't believe he'd so selfishly compromise the house's reputation, not to mention his disregard for the distress he caused the other residents of the house. I took him aside and said, "Bill, how could you do this? There are so many gays out there who have parents who couldn't care less about what their children are doing. Your parents are so genuinely interested in your recovery. Your mother is physically ill. You have traumatized them so much in your twenty-three years of existence. They have gone out of their way to get you the help you need, and you throw it all away for a half-hour clandestine rendezvous with some guy. I can understand where you might fall to sexual temptation, but why you would bring this man to the house is beyond me.

"Did you even realize that if this man knew what this house was all about, and later went to a gay bar and bragged, 'you'll never guess where I had sex this afternoon!' how it could potentially have destroyed the wonderful reputation this ministry has?" I informed him that he had broken one of the cardinal rules of the live-in manual, and that he gave me no other recourse but to dismiss him from the program. With great regret, we had to ship him back to Montana. But that's exactly what he needed. He needed to take responsibility and know that there were serious consequences for his actions. A few years later he called me to let me know that he had come to his senses and was on the road to recovery.

The program that we copied, located in San Francisco, warned us about the pitfalls involved in operating such a program, but in retrospect, we didn't know what we were getting into. Although our intentions were good, we were extremely underfunded and understaffed. Successful programs need at least three staffers per house and must have stringent acceptance criteria. I was naïve enough to believe that anyone who came to us for help was sincere. I didn't realize that some persons would use it as a way to escape from parents, leave bad lover relationships, or to improve their financial stability. One of the roots of homosexuality is envy, and I found that some participants were not willing to do what it takes to recover their heterosexuality and in a jealous, envious way, they even sought to bring down those who were successfully working on their issues.

Looking back on those years, I can say from personal experience that there's quite a difference between seeing an ex-gay once a week for a three-hour support meeting, vs. living with someone "24-7" and realizing the depths of their brokenness and dysfunction. Because many ex-homosexuals are dealing with trust and shame issues, they must first develop trust before they're willing to reveal the depths of their despair. I think that if someone offered me a life-long free prescription for Valium, I *might* attempt a live-in recovery program someday; however I don't recommend undertaking a commitment of this magnitude without first preparing for the vast responsibilities that it entails.

I don't mean to paint a discouraging picture; there were successes in the short two and a half-year history of the program, and I firmly believe that the basic format works. My advice to anyone who might want to open a live-in house is to have at least three in-house counselors per eight residents. Ex-homosexuals can be very secretive and manipulative, and they'll often use the divide and conquer approach to buck authority. It's very important that the leadership stands united when problems arise.

Many ex-gays were accustomed to approaching mommy when daddy said no; they had learned an unhealthy way to get what they want, and in many instances this pattern has continued into adulthood. Therefore this behavior must be confronted if it is to be broken.

As Dr. Elizabeth Moberly states very clearly in her book, *Homosexuality: A New Christian Ethic*, **homosexuals' problem is not with the *opposite* gender; the problem is an underlying ambivalence towards one's *own* gender that leads to the behavior**. Therefore, a male homosexual will experience feelings of ambivalence towards his same-sex counselor, who is in a position of authority over him, especially in a live-in environment. The homosexual will most likely have issues of transference, in which the homosexual transfers his unresolved issues towards his father onto a male authority figure, i.e., the live-in director. The live-in director must be very secure in his masculinity and when attacked by a resident, must not counter-transfer or take the attack personally. He must be prepared for the out-of-left-field attacks that inevitably will come.

If you are struggling with homosexuality or have been in the lifestyle for a long period of time, I would highly recommend that you apply to an ex-gay live-in program. When one recovers from the homosexual condition, one is, in essence, being "re-parented," and that healing occurs most fully within the confines of a live-in program. Organizations like Love-in-Action, based in Memphis, TN, is a great example of a program that works and that I can confidently recommend. But please, for all involved, make sure that you're pledged to stick with an ex-gay program; commitment to the responsibilities of these programs is crucial to your healing.

I highly recommend a live-in situation for someone who has the time to take a year out of his life to work on his issues more fully and deeply. Being a part of a program such as Love-in-Action literally means putting much of your life – career, family, etc. – on *hold* for a year or more and is probably one of the most serious commitments you can ever make toward healing.

CHAPTER 15

THE BIG M BECOMES THE LITTLE M

A great number of homosexuals (and heterosexuals) are addicted to masturbation. Although mainline Christianity teaches that masturbation is sin, most churches don't even mention the subject from the pulpit. I have even had ministry members say that their ministers said that it was OK to do it. I cannot believe how lax the mainline church has gotten in this area.

The Bible tells us in I Corinthians 6:19 that we are "temples of the Holy Spirit." The word masturbation comes from the Latin phrase which means *to defile with your hands*. Attraction towards masturbation usually begins at the time of puberty. Studies show that children who are sexually molested in pre-pubescence will begin this practice as early as five years of age.

It's very obvious to me after being an addict to this compulsion that one "acts this exercise out because it is a way of comforting oneself in relation to a disruption or agitation in the psyche." Pre-pubescent children will not begin to masturbate naturally. It simply isn't in our make-up. They will begin to practice this kind of aberrant behavior only if they have been traumatized sexually or psychologically.

In regards to adolescents that have recently approached pubescence having a desire to practice masturbation, every teen is susceptible to it. But just because they are susceptible to it does not mean that they should practice it.

Many pastors and theologians say that the Holy Scriptures are silent on this issue. It is partially correct the word masturbation is never mentioned or described in the Bible. The only reference is when Onan "wasted his seed" when he refused to impregnate his dead brother's former wife; however, the New Testament has a lot to say when it talks about fornication. The word *fornication* is not used very much in modern language today. However, when I looked up the definition of it in Webster's dictionary I was quite surprised to read what it said: **the incontinence of unmarried persons.** Then when I looked up the definition of incontinence I found that it meant not restraining the passions or appetites; a person that is unchaste.

The devil is having a wonderful time changing the meaning of words. He is "the author of confusion." If he can warp the understanding of what scripture has to say about the forbiddance of homosexual practice and *other* kinds of heterosexual fornication, he can then move on to the next level of deception: nullifying, toning down and even changing the meaning of words. Once this is accomplished, the entire field of deception is opened to re-interpretation of words. Sin no longer is called sin, and the words that describe sin no longer are fully understood or actualized.

The bottom line is that we are called as Christians to refrain from **all** sexual immorality whether it may be homosexuality, pre-marital intercourse of a heterosexual nature, or masturbation. When that was explained to me very clearly at an Exodus National Conference workshop on <u>Healing from Masturbation</u> taught by Mr. Bob Brown of the Seattle, WA ministry called Metanoia. I experienced a healing from my twenty-year addiction. Remember: The truth will set you free.

All one has to do to experience freedom from life dominating sin is first to acknowledge it as sin, confess it, and ask God to take it away. Remember what James 5:16 says: **"If you confess** your sins to one another, **you will be healed."** However, God cannot release you from life dominating sin until you admit to Him and sometimes other people that it actually is sin. I have counseled over 600 former homosexuals in the last 12 years since I have been in ministry and I can tell you that over 85% of them had an addiction to masturbation, pornography, and now the Internet. Until a prayer of renouncement is said to the Lord and a firm commitment to stop the physical act is adhered to, healing from homosexuality cannot be achieved.

Renouncing my addiction to masturbation was **key** to my healing. After the masturbation stopped, I was able to get in touch with the hurts of my past. I allowed myself to feel the pain and move past it by allowing the Holy Spirit to help me take the pain to the cross of Jesus Christ and then leave it there. The masturbation was a very sophomoric attempt to self-medicate. In the past, every time that I masturbated I was able to drown out the pain and stuff it back down. God was showing me that if I was ever going to be free from homosexual bondage I would have to let the pain come up from the pit of my stomach and out of me and then it could be nailed to the cross.

It has also taught me patience and perseverance, both attributes of God, and to be totally dependent on Him, His Son the living Word, and the Holy Spirit for my sustenance. It has been a terribly painful process, however, very freeing. Many homosexuals think that they are *finally free* when they enter the gay lifestyle. I will admit that for a while that will seem to be true. Especially if they have had to keep their same-sex attractions hidden. However, scripture says, "that sin begins as cobwebs and then becomes chains."

Masturbation is usually one of the first bondages that one gets caught up in as a youth travels down the road towards homosexuality and other sexual aberrations. It is, therefore, usually a very hard addiction to overcome. In Dr Jeff Satinovers book <u>Homosexuality & the Politics of Truth</u> he mentions that as we continue to participate in addictive behavior for periods of time the brain will actually began to make physiological changes to accommodate the addiction. In other words during "ejaculation" the brain secretes endorphins that give us the intense feeling of pleasure during the act. If the brain is used to secreting this hormone for the last say 20 or 30 years everyday of your life (and for some sex addicts 2-3 times per day) then the body may have to experience a "de-tox." That's why masturbation is such a tough addiction to break.

Another reason why people overcoming masturbation have a tough time is that in the spirit realm the devil knows that you have begun the process of healing. Knowing that you are no longer "acting out" with members of the same sex he will try to keep you in your addiction by "whispering things into your head" such as "Go ahead... masturbate...at least you are not acting out with someone else" **or** "Why don't you masturbate now and get it over with...you know that you're going to do it by the end of the day anyhow!" And if he can't get you to "act out" with new people he will try to keep you in bondage with "old re-runs" of former lovers. The "re-runs" will usually involve fantasy and masturbation. And what will happen is that whenever you are feeling lonely, tired or stressed, you will naturally want to "medicate" the situation by returning to masturbation or other forms of stimulation for comfort. To overcome addiction from a purely Christian vantage, one must submit his entire spirit, soul and **body** to the cross of Jesus for crucifixion. That is the only way out of it. Modern therapists can help you change behavior and even worse, liberal therapists can help you "manage sin" or "medicate it." However, if you want truly to heal from a homosexual disorientation, only total crucifixion of bodily desires will qualify you.

The other argument that supports the fact that masturbation is sinful is the truth that during the act one has to ask what one is thinking about while in the midst of masturbation? Typically he is usually fantasizing about other men. How do you expect to recover from an addiction to men if you continually idolize them during the actual act and then shortly afterwards experience the intense gratification of ejaculation while looking at an airbrushed picture of the "ideal" man?

If you are already struggling with low self-esteem, do you think it's going to help lift your view of your own masculinity by fantasizing about someone who has been airbrushed into perfection by a computer? How could your psyche possibly compete with that?

The Bruno Story

God has a great sense of humor. One of the ways that he showed me that my homosexuality was fueled by low self-esteem based in fantasy and idolatry was the Bruno Story. Bruno was a big porno-star of the 1970's in gay films. He was exceptionally handsome and muscular, with dark Italian features. He was the **idol** of just about every gay who watched porno films. I always tried to convince myself that "if I could only have Bruno as my boyfriend, my life would be complete. I would be happy for the rest of my life and I would never have to look at another guy again."

Then sometime in the mid-70's, I finally had the opportunity to meet him. David, who was my best gay friend and bar buddy, had been to Fire Island the past weekend and had the opportunity to meet Bruno at a gay cocktail party. He told him about me and that I was dying to meet him. Bruno seemed interested and then agreed to meet me in the Village the following weekend. I couldn't believe it. As I was thanking David profusely for this incredible opportunity he stopped me in mid-sentence and said; "Before you get too excited, there are some things that I have to tell you about him." I said "O.K. what?" He said; "To begin with, do you know how all of the porno films portray him as a construction worker, policeman, etc?" I then said, "Yeah, well what does he really do for a living?" He reluctantly informed me that he was a reservationist for Eastern Airlines! My heart sank a little, but I recovered and said, "Who cares? I can live with that."

Mark then dropped the next bomb and told me that Bruno wasn't his real name. I then said, "I don't care… what is it?" **He said, "Herman!"** Then he added, "And it gets a little worse. Do you know that tough deep voice that he speaks in on all his videos…well that's a voice over. He actually has a squeaky, high-pitched voice."

Again I couldn't believe it! **I had been in lust for seven years with an airline reservationist from New Jersey with a high squeaky voice named Herman!** My eyes were opening to the reality of just how deeply the gay sub-culture is immersed in illusion and fantasy.

If one is ever to recover his heterosexuality, he must overcome his idolatrous thoughts of other men based mainly in fantasy. If you are involved with masturbation, Internet addiction to porno sites and chat rooms, these must go! The porno magazines and "running" magazines have to be thrown out! God will reveal to you in His time the truth and reality…That you are made in His image, that you don't need pictures of other men to feel complete, that you are not a mistake, that muscles and a beard do not make a man, nor does having knowledge and data of every football team in the NFL!

True masculinity is having a right relationship with Jesus and the Father. It means living your life chastely until he brings you a bride. True manliness is saving yourself for one woman in the boundaries of holy matrimony or living as a celibate single, if that is what God has called you to do.

God did call me to marriage; and when I made a covenant with Him to give up the different manifestations of idolatry that had crept into my life, then and only then did my heterosexuality fully begin to kick in. It was absolutely crucial to my healing process. God was truly restoring the times that the locust had eaten out of my life.

What was even more incredible was that the sexual attraction toward my wife began to increase and my envy of men began to wane. I couldn't believe that it was happening. God answered my prayers because I showed Him that I was serious and obedient to His word.

Postscript: Please do a word study in your Bible on such terms as *chaste, pure, holy, body, sexual, purity, eunuch, fornication and immorality*. It will help you to understand God's desire for our earthly bodies.

CHAPTER 16

IF YOU HAVE A LOVED ONE WHO IS GAY: HELP FOR FAMILIES

I really do wish that I had the time and energy to write an entire book on the subject of how the affected family members can offer a proper Christian response to their loved ones announcement of their homosexuality. I know how devastating this could be. I have ministered to hundreds of parents, siblings, co-workers and now (unfortunately) children of homosexuals. I have felt their pain, and have heard their cries for help. The ex-gay movement seems to be providing adequate coverage for the struggling homosexual; however, in my opinion, Parents & Friends Ministries is the only ministry that is providing adequate Christ-centered outreach to the affected family members. For many years the families of alcoholics suffered silently until their loved ones reached out to Alcoholics Anonymous (AA) for help. But families of alcoholics soon realized that whether their loved one continued to drink or not, *they* needed help for themselves. And in the same vein, whether your loved one has decided to leave the lifestyle or not, you should reach out and get some help from Parents & Friends Ministries in West Palm Beach, Florida. Please check out our website at **parentsandfriends.20m**.com We can plug you into a national network of others like yourselves who will offer you a shoulder to cry on, some hope and then a plan of attack!

We are the Al-anon of the ex-gay movement. But we have not yet been able to scratch the surface of the level of needs of these families and friends. Financial constraints and staff size have been limiting us. The mainline Church, Christian family protection organizations and counseling centers could be doing much more. How can we tell woman not to have an abortion without providing crisis pregnancy counseling? And in the same vein, how can we tell homosexuals not to be gay if we are not offering proper Christ-centered support to them, I'm not talking about little makeshift offices stuck in some corner of a church somewhere where when a desperate soul calls for help they'll get an answering machine. I'm speaking about properly staffed and funded counseling venues all over the country where homosexuals and their families may come and receive help. Sometimes I head home from my office at the end of the day exhausted, and cry out to the Lord, "Please help us!" I wait for the day when the church and all these Christian family organizations are going to come to our aid. I have been involved in the ex-gay movement for over eighteen years and have seen many of my colleagues' burn out from exhaustion, not because they were involved in a ministry that was not "a call" on their lives, but because they were so overworked and underpaid.

There have even been leaders in the ex-gay movement who have fallen back into the lifestyle because they had moved out into ministry "before their time" (before they had worked through their own issues). They saw the great need for outreach, realized that no one else was getting involved, so with the compassion that was in their heart for their fellow-strugglers, they reached out prematurely and fell flat on their faces. In reality, it is the healthy that should be helping the needy, not the individuals that are still dealing with their own healing process! How tragic!

I believe that when we all come before the Lord in judgment someday, He will be more merciful to many of the gay community who have given of themselves to the many different AIDS causes than to some of these Christian "celebrities" or church officials who point a finger at the gay movement but do little or nothing to relieve the pain of the AIDS victim or the homosexual struggler. Jesus said, "When you do this to the least of my brother's you do this to me."

There is a Mother Theresa AIDS hospice in Washington, DC that the Sisters of Charity run. A dear friend of mine, who is a medical doctor, volunteers her time there. She told me once that over 97% of the men they minister to "get themselves right" with the Lord before they die.

Although the sisters don't make any apologies for the Church's stand on the homosexual issue, they are not judgmental. They will take care of the men, feed them, change their diapers (when they become incontinent), but at the same time will be praying that they will give their wills over to the Lord Jesus. It is the love of Jesus that the volunteers emulate that brings these strugglers to the cross.

The devil is offering the homosexual hamburger, and when he is hungry, he'll eat anything. The Church needs to be offering the homosexual *filet mignon*. The average homosexual has been propagandized by the gay activists into believing that the Christian Church is their enemy. We must overcome these lies with the Truth. The Truth is that Jesus came to set the captives free, and with God anything is possible.

They need to hear that we, like Jesus, love them, *not* the sin that they are involved in, but *them*. We need to tell them that He died to overcome *whatever* binds up their heart.

We must not be condemning but must be careful that we are not practicing *sloppy agape love*. There are many parishes and congregations that are practicing "menu-Christianity." Choose what *you* want to believe.

Many churches sometimes want to offer to be the doctor but are deathly afraid to administer the **proper** medicine. When a boil is oozing pus, a band-aid is not going to handle the situation. If the boil is going to heal, it must first be lanced. Then the infection must be washed out with alcohol (and heaven knows this will burn) and *then* the healing can begin.

Being a "doctor" of ex-gays is not an easy task. It's not for the squeamish or the faint of heart. Being a family member or friend who would like to help a loved one exit the lifestyle involves a full commitment of time. And once you plan your strategy and implement it, there is no turning back. You might have to regroup and adjust your battle plan sometimes, but you must never retreat.

Now that we have discussed the problem, let's look at some solutions. When your loved one drops the bomb, **do not** overreact! And if you've overreacted already (in most instances) there is still time to admit that you made a mistake and apologize. The devil is just waiting for you to reject your loved one, so that he or she will come running to him. It's hard to hear, but the gay community is quite organized and in many instances will be the "safety net" that your gay loved one will run to for comfort. **Avoid this at all costs!** Sometimes if the wrong thing is said, this may alienate the homosexual from his/her family for a period of many years.

It's OK to cry when he or she breaks the news. Your homosexual loved one needs to know that you are hurt and concerned. Don't hold back the tears. Please be aware that there are over twelve "self-help" books on the market, carefully orchestrated by gay activists, that teach your children or other loved ones how to "break the news" to the family. I suggest that you purchase one of these books so that you will know when you are being manipulated or subjected to other similar tactics that are mentioned in these books.

The books are very cleverly written to make the parents feel guilty into accepting the homosexual's lifestyle. They will use canned statements such as "I am still your son/daughter/friend. Nothing has changed," or "How could you possibly love me if you don't accept my lifestyle /boyfriend / girlfriend?" If this manipulation is delivered, a good response would be; "I can still continue to love you, nothing will ever change that, but at the same time strongly disagree with the lifestyle that you are planning on living. I am more concerned as your parent/loved one in giving you proper advice that will affect where you will spend eternity then to remain popular with you."

You must stand united as husband/wife and/or family. If your loved one is cunning, he/she will try to divide you. Remember that the Bible says that a divided house will fall. If he/she sees that you have not rejected him/her but know it will be a cold day in hell before you consider accepting an invitation to meet the "lover," he/she will know **immediately** that certain boundaries are set and **are not moveable.**

Maybe you haven't been the best parent in the world. Maybe you have been too wishy-washy in regards to the way that you have disciplined or maybe you have been too much of a disciplinarian. This does not, however, excuse you from exercising your continual duties as parents. Even if you haven't been the best parents in the world, nothing is stopping you from beginning this noble task today! Start out by setting the guidelines of tolerance **and do not retreat**! Many homosexuals are typically manipulative, *spoiled*, and used to having their own way. Parents, don't give in!

In many instances, parents will find out about their children's gay leanings not because they were told but because they might have discovered some porno in the child's room or on the Internet. Or a carelessly-left-out love letter might be discovered. In regards to this, I have no problem with the parents' making a further inspection of the room/house. If you suspect that your loved one is a homosexual and know that you will be having a face-to-face confrontation, you are going to need hard tangible evidence, or Johnny or Suzy might try to deny your allegations. If you have tangible evidence, your position will be hard to thwart. If he/she accuses you of being too nosy or says something like, "how dare you go into my room or onto my computer; this is none of your business," don't fall for the guilt trip. Your answer should be, "You are my son/daughter/ loved one, when my discernment tells me that you, whom I love very much, are in trouble, I will do whatever I have to do to make sure that you are OK. I love you too much! I will not stick my head into the sand. If that bothers you…I'm sorry!"

Should You Invite Your Child's Boyfriend Home for Christmas Dinner?

I have been involved in ministry to former homosexuals and their families for nearly eighteen years. I have also met and counseled many parents, and the question that many parents ask is: "My son wants to bring his boyfriend home for Christmas dinner with our family. Do you think that this is a good idea?" After much thought, prayer, seeking God and reading Scripture, I have come to the conclusion that **this is not something I could recommend**. Many parents feel guilty about some of the mistakes that they have made in their children's upbringing. They might have been over-bearing, psychologically absent, physically or verbally abusive, non-confrontational, etc. You must come to grips with the reality that you may have made some mistakes in your child's upbringing, and it may have led them further down the path to homosexuality. However, if you have confessed these sins to God through confession and others in your local PFM meeting or church accountability group, then you are forgiven. **Stop living under the guilt of shame!** By no means allow your child to manipulate you because of your guilt. Just because you have not been the best parents sometimes because of naivete` or circumstances beyond your control does not mean that you must remain in patterns that will continue to hurt your child and affect his healing process! Proverbs 27:5 states very clearly: **"Open reproof is better than voiceless love."** Don't remain under the cloud of guilt after you have confessed your sin and/or shortcomings.

From here on in, old, bad parenting patterns are behind you. Your children will see you in a new light. No more of the weak father or emotionally incestuous mother who is afraid to be a strong parent. From here on, your house will be a Christ-centered home with proper boundaries. Your child will start to get the parenting and discipline he should have received years ago instead of the voiceless love that many children receive.

Having the strength to "just say no" is what your child who is still in the homosexual lifestyle needs. Kids (and adult children) need LSD (Love, Security and Discipline). If you won't discipline your child, then you are not showing him or her love. Even God chastises the ones He loves. My parents knew about my homosexuality and were somewhat accepting, but they did set some boundaries (that I rebelled against, but in the long run appreciated). I knew that by not living in their house, I was free to live the wild lifestyle that I had chosen. But, when I came home for Christmas and other holidays, I knew that the fantasy world I was living in had to come to an abrupt stop as I entered their front door. In the long run, it was one of the realities that helped me leave the lifestyle behind. From my secret "lifestyle" I entered the reality of real family life, mortgages, children, budgets, church and heterosexuality. I now realize that it also kept me somewhat anchored and kept me from "cutting the anchor" totally away from the ship".

A parent of a homosexual will often say to me, "If I don't allow him to bring his boyfriend home, he told me that he will not come home for Christmas, either." After she utters this statement, I have to inform her painfully that she had *already* lost her child years ago when he entered the lifestyle. Parents must realize that the child that they knew in their early years is now capable of lying, manipulating and deceiving in a way that they never thought would have been possible.

Homosexual children, once they have given in to the lure of the gay subculture, are capable of sneaking pornography into the house, gay web sites, involving themselves with secret bouts of masturbation under your roof, calling 900 numbers from your phone, even having sex in your house (whether you are at home or not). You must stand strong and keep your home a Holy sanctuary. Inviting your child's sexual partner to your home sends a mixed message. In one breath you are saying that you do not approve of his lifestyle choice, and in the next you are confusing him by allowing his boyfriend in for turkey dinner! Please read 1 Corinthians 5:9-12 where it warns us not to associate with people (who call themselves believers) that are sexually immoral. It hits really close to home when this person happens to be our son or daughter. It's a very hard decision to make, but it must be made.

If you child wants to come home for a visit alone, **encourage it** so that lines of communication remain open, remembering that you have the responsibility to set the limits of his or her visit.

Personally, if I had my cake and I could eat it too, I don't think that I would ever have had been motivated to leave the gay life behind. Sometimes I remember being able to manipulate my parents into doing something that pushed my gayness upon them.

I really wish that they had been stronger with me and had addressed my manipulative tactics.

Deep inside, I was dying for the discipline. I will repeat again, these days the organized gay community has books on how to manipulate your parents into accepting your homosexuality.

Parents! Do not give in to these calculated tactics.

I remember being at my twin brother's wedding. I was still in the lifestyle at the time, and I saw my brother up there on the altar with his future bride. I remember that a voice in my head kept saying to me "if you don't leave the gay lifestyle behind, you will never experience the fullness of having a wife and children." I was living what I used to think was an exciting life, but deep down inside I knew that I was terribly lonely. I wanted what my brother had and wanted to be married with children. God used another one of my "reality days at home" to show me what I was truly missing. If my parents had told me to come to the wedding and bring Biff, I probably would have lost out on a good opportunity to learn a good life lesson.

Another opportunity to receive from the Lord came through a painful life experience when one of my brothers died suddenly when I was in my early 20's. I remember leaving the church after the funeral mass. We had hired some limousines for the occasion, and as the chauffeurs were assigning different family members to their cars, I observed each of my brothers getting into his respective car with his wife. When it came my turn to occupy a car, the chauffeur said to me, "Hey, why don't you just sit up front with me?" It affected me terribly that each of my brothers had someone to share his grief with but that I was all alone. God will use many different life-situations to convict us so that He may gain our attention.

As parents we sometimes want to shield our children from pain and suffering that God may want to use to transform their lives. We must not stand in God's way. **Many times we want to be our children's savior, and we must realize that only God can save them.** Scripture says very clearly in John 6:44 that **only He can draw us to His Son.** We must not stand in the way. God can use us as His instruments, but we must not take His job from Him; the consequences can be disastrous.

Pray God's will for your child and trust that the Lord knows better. He does not want to see your child delivered over to the flames of hell for continuing to live an immoral lifestyle. It is His desire for him or her to be saved. Through exercising Christian discipline in your home (even if it's late), you can help guide your child in seeing the error of his or her ways. He must learn the difference between right and wrong. You must not send mixed signals. And most important, if you see your prodigal child running down the road toward your house someday in repentance, run down and pick him or her up in your arms and welcome him or her home.

Give your child over to the Lord and don't steal him back. Ask God in your prayers to do whatever it takes to get through to him/her, even if it's on a deathbed. Scripture tells us that **"we should not be concerned about the body, for the body is temporal. We should be concerned about the soul, because it is eternal."**

If you are interested in hearing more about this subject please contact our West Palm Beach office at (561) 655-3055 and purchase a copy of the video Should I Invite My Child's Lover Home for Christmas Dinner? It's very helpful in answering any further questions that you may have on this topic.

CHAPTER 17

HOW THE CHURCH CAN HELP

When I speak of the Church, I am referring to the main-line traditional bible-believing spirit-filled congregations that represent the fragmented Body of Christ. In my opinion, we will come into full communion with each other in these "last days." The Lord Jesus Christ prays in John 15:5-8 "that they may **all** be one as we are one so that the world may know that You have sent **them.**" I also believe firmly that whatever Jesus prayed to the Father will come to be (because He always is in the Father's will). Thus, with that understanding, when I mention the Church, it is that to which I am referring.

Just as the previous chapter warns the parents to be united in this battle for their children's souls, so must the Church come together to join this fight. We obviously need the power of the Holy Spirit to come up against the evil that has dragged some of the most wonderfully gifted creations of God into this lifestyle that is killing them physically and eventually spiritually.

The only denomination that has an official ex-gay ministry available is the Methodists. Their ex-gay network is called Transforming Congregations, which has about fifty chapters and is based in Bakersfield, California.

The two ex-gay networks called Homosexuals Anonymous (H.A.) and Exodus are non-denominational. H.A. has about fifty chapters, which are mainly located in the United States, and is based in Reading, Pennsylvania. However, most of its annual budget of $72K comes from its members. The mainline Protestant church is not supporting H.A. enough, although it is doing Christ-like work. Because of the lack of support, H.A. is able to employ only two full-time persons on their national staff. Many of these national organizations depend on volunteer staff, or they wouldn't be able to respond to the thousands of calls that come into their offices each year.

Exodus has about ninety chapters and is also primarily member-supported. They have about ten full-time staff people in their national office and have an annual budget of around $1,000,000. It also depends on a large number of volunteers. Most of these organizations are being held together by the faith of their founders and supporters; sometimes this can be a very heavy burden to carry.

All of these organizations including the organization that I founded named Parents & Friends Ministries with offices located in West Palm Beach, Florida need the prayers and financial support of the mainline church and it's members if they are going to survive.

Now that we have introduced the five ex-gay networks; Parents & Friends Ministries (PFM), Courage, Homosexuals Anonymous(H.A.),ExodusandTransformingCongregations, the different Churches and their members need to ask them-selves how they can help relieve some of the burdens that these organizations have carried for far too long. The first suggestion that I have is for the Church to give some imme-diate financial support to these ex-gay networks. Different ministries around the country continue to close their doors because of a lack of funding and staff. One can only imagine the amount of spiritual warfare these ministries experience.

Secondly, the ex-gay movement needs to be publicly embraced by the Church. We are providing Christ-centered outreach to a group of people that the Lord Jesus loves very much. This movement is still considered a "leper ministry" by most Christians.

A certain well-known family protection organization recently told PFM that they were really behind us; however, one day when we really needed to use their pressroom for a media briefing that we were hosting, they wouldn't allow it. They were afraid to be considered too closely allied with us because of the retaliation that they *might* experience from the gay activists.

The politically motivated "churches" are currently winning the battle for the soul of America. The gay "churches" such as the Metropolitan Community Church, the pro-gay (sloppy agape) liberal church and the Unitarians (who really don't teach all of what mainline Christianity believes) are doing a better job of bringing homosexuals into **their** folds then the true Church. This is outrageous and must change.

They (the false churches) are spending millions of dollars on homosexuals to keep them in bondage. **We are not doing our job,** and I fear the Lord God is going to be "ticked off." Remember the admonition in Romans 10:14-15 that says, "How then are they to call on Him if they had not come to believe in Him? And how can they believe in Him **if they have never heard of Him?** And how will they hear of Him **unless there is a preacher for them?** And how will there be preachers if they are not sent?" As scripture further says: *"How beautiful are the feet of the messengers of Good News."*

The clock is ticking, time is running out, people are dying due to lack of knowledge, people are dying because the love of the Christian community has not been evident to the average homosexual. Most of the ex-gays I know came out of homosexuality because a Christian had the *audacity* to treat them with respect and took the time to show them what God's Word really has to say about homosexuality.

Unfortunately many Christians really do believe deep down inside that to change someone's sexual orientation is just too big for God. Isn't it sad that they can believe that God made the Atlantic Ocean and healed Aunt Sophie's cancer, but that the Holy Spirit can't heal some childhood wounds that led someone into the gay lifestyle?

Many people in the Church have been fed the propaganda of the very well funded gay political lobbyist. They have over $150 million dollars a year to spend on lobbying America into believing that homosexuals are "born that way," and they have been quite successful.

If there is any question in your mind as to whether God allows someone to be born gay or not, just remember what scripture has to say about it in I Corinthians 6:9-11: Do you not realize that people who do evil will never inherit the kingdom of God? Do not be deceived- the sexually immoral, idolaters, adulterers, the self-indulgent, sodomites, thieves, misers, drunkards, slanderers and swindlers; none of these will inherit the kingdom of God. Some of you used to be of that kind: but you have been washed clean, you have been sanctified, and you have been justified in the name of the Lord Jesus Christ and through the Holy Spirit. **If God tells us that practicing homosexuals will never enter the kingdom of God, then don't you think that it would be very cruel if God brought us into the world condemned to hell already?** Everyone has an opportunity to obtain salvation.

You must never believe that homosexuals are born that way. There has never been any evidence to prove such a statement, and I think a biological cause will never be found. But that will not stop the Evil One from trying to deceive you into thinking that homosexuality is innate. Always believe the Word of God over what you read in the newspapers. If what you read in the newspaper is in conflict with Holy Scripture, **don't believe it!**

Once you are convinced that change is possible, you need to open up your arms and your local congregation to the repentant homosexual. Find out where the closest ex-gay ministry is, contact the director and offer him whatever "talents" the Lord has given you, whether it's gifts of administration, hospitality, finances, computer skills, prayer support, time, advertising skills, public relations, etc.

This movement needs to grow and has so many needs. Just show-up at a local chapter and take the director out to lunch. God will reveal to you how you can help. It might be a simple thing such as answering phone calls, sending out mailings or being an ever-straight encourager to an ex-gay. Just show-up. You will be greatly appreciated.

Sponsor a weekend seminar on healing for the homosexual. Many local chapters of the five ex-gay networks are well equipped to present a seminar to your local congregation. This is typically the best way to get your fellow church members involved. It also is a great vehicle for healing "homophobia" in your local church home. We must realize that the gay political movement in this country has given America a false impression of what the gay world is really like. Many persons in your local church body might be under the impression that welcoming ex-gays means to accept the gay lifestyle within your church.

They might even have fear that they will catch AIDS by just touching someone who is gay, or that all homosexuals are child molesters; and if they come into their church it will put their young congregation at risk. No one can say for certain if anyone is ever going to touch a child in your congregation. I would certainly be concerned about it. I would not put an ex-gay in children's ministry until the priest/pastor who is counseling this individual feels comfortable doing so; however, many homosexuals that have been victims of sexual abuse as a child wouldn't *think* of touching a child in an unholy manner. They know the grief that their personal molestation caused them and would not engage in such an action.

A simple way to get the word out that there is help for the repentant homosexual is to hand out multiple copies of the local ministry's newsletter. With the permission of your pastor, place the newsletter within the Sunday bulletin.

Maybe you might be interested in being pro-active by accompanying some of the members of the local ministry to a gay march or to the gay bars at night to hand out tracts of information. That can be a very good way to be pro-active in your community. Please make sure, however, that you have been properly trained on the specifics of reaching out in a potentially volatile territory. The local ministry director, if he has a call in this area, would be a good resource for the do's and don'ts of street ministry.

And last, but not least, please consider being an **ever-straight encourager** to someone that is going through healing. As you probably know by now, most homosexuals in their early childhood usually did not bond with their same-sex parent. As part of the recovery-process, they are asked to disclose their struggle to a same-sex member of their local parish/congregation in order to develop a healthy account-ability/peer relationship with that person. This usually involves a commitment of time and should not be under-taken unless you are serious. In essence you will be used by the Lord to re-parent that individual or become a role model of masculinity or femininity for them.

This task, if accepted, can have a major impact on the ex-gays healing process and move it along quickly. You must be prepared however for the spiritual warfare that surrounds this task, and you must also be very secure in your own sexual identity. If you are too concerned over what others might think about your having a desire to assist an ex-gay by befriending him, then you probably shouldn't accept this challenge.

Everyone knows how gossip can spread around a church and if your masculinity or femininity cannot handle some mean-spirited false allegations, then don't get involved. Remember: you do not need man's approval; you need God's. Even after some training from the local director, you may feel a little unprepared. Just remember God will be with you; and if you don't have all the answers, ask for some help. I can tell you that this is some of the most rewarding work that a mature Christian can undertake. I have seen many persons recover for whom I have been an encourager. And to attend their wedding or receive a birth announcement in the mail when they have brought forth their first child is among the most exciting and joyous occasions that I have ever experienced in my life.

Use your imagination; I'm sure that the Holy Spirit will give you plenty of other ideas that will properly suit each specific situation. It isn't so hard as you may think. Just have a desire to see God's will carried out in that former-homosexual's life and watch what He will do.

CHAPTER 18

WHAT THE EX-GAY MOVEMENT MUST ACCOMPLISH TO SUCCEED

The Lord God has a great sense of humor. If I had known what I was getting myself into when I accepted this call, I don't know if I would have accepted the challenge. Do I love my work…Yes? Is it very hard? Do I sometimes want to just give it all up and open-up a smart little gift shop in the suburbs? We must realize however that we have been bought with a price and that we are not our own. **We must go where the Lord sends us**.

We must also realize that to whom much is given, much is expected. I have been preserved from physical *and* spiritual death to bring glory to God, and if it is His choice for me to be involved in this very tough life-adventure, so be it.

I would be lying if I told you that this has been an easy cross to bear, I think that after reading this book you have probably come to the same conclusion. But I can tell you that I am just where the Lord wants me; however, the scripture in Exodus 12:5 comes to mind when Moses cries out, "Why did you give me this stubborn and obstinate people."

Being involved with ex-gay ministry and all the vitriolic spiritual warfare that accompanies it isn't a piece of cake. Or when you preach your heart out (hinting to the congregation of some acute ministry needs) and some lady in a fur coat hands you a check for $5.

Unity of the Five Ex-gay Networks

The fundraising debacle is one of the greatest obstacles that needs to be overcome if this movement is ever going to succeed. But more important the five ex-gay networks need to work more cohesively with each other. The same situation exists in the ex-gay movement that exists in the Christian church in general: discord. This movement must be unified! There are so many enemies from without, we do not need them from within!

Then we move to the next level of dysfunction in the church when one hears things like, "Your ex-gay group is too charismatic... and yours isn't charismatic enough! Our group believes in healing and your group believes only in abstinence. You've got to do Andy Comisky's Living Water Program or you won't heal. Andy's Living Waters Program is California Christianity. LeAnne Payne is one of the Godliest women alive...LeAnne Payne is a witch!"

The Lord says in John 17:21..."I pray, Father, **that they may all be one as we are one**, so that the world may know **that you have sent them.**" The Church and the ex-gay movement must exhibit this oneness. If we continue to be stubborn and don't settle our differences, the Lord will bring about this unity by allowing us to be persecuted. This will quickly bring unity. And we must not forget if Jesus prayed it, it will most certainly happen. I don't like to see the Body of Christ divided, and, more important, neither does our Lord Jesus.

I believe that the Lord is going to use my life experiences and testimony to help bring the end-time unity of the Body of Christ. I have been on all sides of this argument and the Lord has allowed me to see just how fragmented His Church really is. I have seen the "wheat and the tares" in all of the Christian camps.

Scripture tells us that you will know the real Christians by their fruits. I have seen the phony Christians and the real ones on all levels of Christianity. I have seen the dead congregations and parishes, apostate denominations, pseudo-Christian denominations, Pharisaic leaders, and clergy that are wolf in sheep's clothing and it grieves my soul.

Local Church Involvement

If the ex-gay movement is going to flourish, it needs to attach itself more closely to the local parishes and congregations. I see a time when ex-gay support groups and parent groups will be meeting at the local parish of every community. The local regional office for a denomination needs to fund the expenses necessary to set-up a substantial ex-gay outreach that is in relation to the size of the gay population of that region.

I pray that Rome especially with the recent sex-scandals coming out of Boston will start to help the many priests and lay people who are struggling with unwanted same-sex desires. We can't expect to keep our eyes closed any longer. It's time to roll-up our sleeves and attack this evil head-on.

I pray that the bishops will begin to clean up the sexual immorality that has plagued its seminaries for far too long. If priests, seminarians, and other religious leaders continue to preach the pro-gay theology and sometimes practice it themselves, if they will not repent and change their ways, then they must be defrocked, denied ordination, or excommunicated.

It's also time to start using the "Big E Word" again. I know of a certain Catholic senator from Boston, Massachusetts who needs to receive a long-overdue warning of excommunication from Rome. His public support of homosexuality in Washington, DC is scandalous.

A National Ex-gay Clearinghouse and Counseling Center

I would love to serve on a board of a national ex-gay Information and Clearinghouse Center. The gay movement is light-years ahead of us in this area. Can you imagine a 1-800 number that any troubled youth, homosexual, or family member could call to find out what kind of ex-gay support is available to them within their area. And with that there should be a 24-hotline offering around the clock crisis counseling.

Public Relations and Lobbying

There also needs to be a large public-relations center based out of a media center such as Washington, DC, New York or Los Angeles. There is a plethora of issues directly or indirectly related to homosexual issues. Having an Ex-gay Public Relations Office in a major city would enable us to be a resource for the media when they need a conservative authoritative response to an issue that is morally based.

The ex-gay movement should have been more of a part of the current-event debates over such topics as whether gays should be allowed to serve as leaders in the Boy Scouts, gay marriage, AIDS legislation, and prevention. It should also be involved with the debate over whether gays should be allowed to have special rights in the workplace, i.e., the Employment Non-discrimination Act (ENDA), gay adoption, sexual abuse and pedophilia legislation.

It's very disconcerting to live in Washington, DC and hear about the different committee hearings held in Washington everyday to discuss moral issues that indirectly touch on the issue of homosexuality. Bob Knight, now at Media Research Institute, has tried a number of times to get some of the more prominent ex-gays onto these special committees to offer expert testimony and advice. But the gay lobbyists have Capitol Hill so tied up and in their back pocket that we do not get a chance an invitation to comment on important legislation that our life experiences could illuminate.

Visibility and Limited Political Involvement
Until the incredible media campaign that caught the gay movement and the media by surprise in 1998 was launched, the ex-gay movement was one of the best-kept secrets in the world. Why was that? The ex-gay movement holds a major key to bringing down a sexual revolution that has nearly destroyed the Judeo-Christian moral fiber of America since it began in the early 1960's. **We are the ultimate sexual abstinence program. Our healing and recovery programs are great ways that could help end the AIDS pandemic tomorrow!** This movement has been around for over a quarter of a century. Why isn't it better known? I've been challenging the ex-gay movement since the mid 90's to have the first Ex-gay March on Washington. It would cause a media panic. They wouldn't know how to contain ten thousand ex-gays marching down the great Washington Mall chanting…"We're here, We're ex-queer. Get used to it!"

The ex-gay national offices should be in prominent media centers and not in Orlando, Bakersfield, or Reading. **We have a visibility problem**. We need to be where the rest of the country can hear more about us! We need to open a National Ex-gay Office in Washington, DC!

Some persons who have been caught in the web of homosexuality are among the brightest, most gifted persons that I have ever met. The gay political community has no problem tapping into their brilliance, and we as the ex-gay community shouldn't either. Some of the many ex-gays I have met have the capability to help change the world. Their genius needs to be tapped and unleashed. The possibilities are unlimited. The U.S. Government, the Christian political-family protection organizations, the Churches and the legal network haven't figured this out yet. **We are the trump card that has yet to be played!**

We are here waiting patiently to answer the call; however, we are not being taken seriously. This must change before it's too late for America. We have the knowledge and the wisdom to push back the gay political agenda in America. We could annihilate their propagandistic campaign of destruction within two years if we were given the opportunity and the resources.

Resource Center

Parents & Friends Ministries of West Palm Beach, Florida opened the first ex-gay retail bookstore in the country called the St. Augustine's Sexual Healing Bookstore when it was located in Washington, DC. The public can walk in off the street and purchase books on sexually healing and recovery from over 100 titles. We offered free educational material, tracts of information, videotapes, testimonies, audiotapes and CD's. We are now preparing a website that will offer all of this material with the click of a mouse-button. The possibilities are limitless. We have developed a prototype bookstore that can be easily reproduced all over the world, opened with less than $40,000, using only 400 square feet of retail space. I have a vision of seeing these sexual healing bookstores opening all over the country...all over the world, offering help to the heterosexual who is sexually broken.

Billboard Campaign

Can you imagine driving down Route 1 of Anytown, U.S.A. and seeing a larger-than-life bulletin board screaming in bold letters something like: ARE YOU SICK AND TIRED OF THE GAY LIFESTYLE...THERE IS HOPE! or YOU CAN LOVE YOUR HOMOSEXUAL CHILD, YET DISAGREE WITH HIS LIFESTYLE CHOICE! This media campaign can be target marketed to gay neighborhoods such as Castro, The Village, South Beach, or Dupont Circle. This could literally bring tens of thousands of homosexuals and lesbians out of the lifestyle. The gay community and the media can no longer deny that the ex-gay movement is here to stay; so, the next strategy that they have developed is a smear and slander campaign. They even have an employee at the Human Rights Campaign Fund (HRCF) whose function is to find gay people who abandoned their healing process and have returned to the lifestyle. He then parades their abandoned attempt in front of the gay political community, using them in a lame attempt to prove that because **they didn't make it out the lifestyle, no one can.** The great majority of gay persons now know that the ex-gay movement exists, and ever so cautiously they've been observing this movement. The gay political lobbyists know this also and are doing their best to extinguish any glimmer of hope in the gay community that healing is possible. That's why a billboard media campaign bringing our message directly to the homosexual community (where the gay lobbyists can't put their spin on it) would be very powerful and could change the direction of this battle.

Fundraising

Having the Holy Spirit's blessing and protection is the most important component that must be in place if the ex-gay movement is to succeed. Accepting this as a given, the movement's next most need is adequate funding. The ex-gay movement is still considered a "leper" ministry by the organized Body of Christ. People will give money to help alcoholics, drug addicts, and women in crisis pregnancies, but there seems to be a taboo against giving to this movement.

The "H"-word still makes people cringe. Speaking honestly, the Church still doesn't fully believe that God is bigger than this "gay thing." The gay politicos have done a marvelous job of convincing America that "they are born this way." It's alarming that some good Christians have bought the lie.

Part of the ex-gay movement's mission, surprisingly, has been to educate the Church on just how powerful the blood of Jesus *really is*. Christians come up to us all the time and make remarks such as, "I didn't know God can change a homosexual," or "That's one of the most amazing testimonies I have ever heard." They really think that this is incredible (and virtually impossible). Because it happened to me, I obviously don't have a problem believing it; however, I often have to quote scriptures such as "with God *anything* is possible!" to churched Christians. People need to be encouraged to believe that God's miracles are for today and can heal the wounded soul.

I am a visionary, *but* this movement cannot ride on air! This vision cannot come to fruition without a concerted effort by the Church. A full response of the Church body will involve a great financial commitment, powerful prayer and intercession, volunteerism, sharing of resources, unity and a whole "lotta" chutzpah! Will you join me in this noble task? Come join this glorious battle for souls that Jesus allowed His body to be pierced for. Remember, when the last name written in the Lamb's Book of Life is saved, then He will come in glory. I believe that many of those names are to be found in the homosexual community. This remnant is precious to the Lord.

EPILOGUE

We are living in perilous times. The battle lines have been drawn. The evil one is no longer hiding his ugly fangs. The book of Revelation 3:15-16 says, "I know about your activities: how you are neither cold nor hot. I wish that you were one or the other, but since you are neither cold or hot, but only lukewarm, I will spit you out of my mouth." When I *really* gave my heart over to the Lord Jesus and began to become a serious student of the Bible, this piece of scripture really convicted me.

I started out my adult life under the false-impression that I could live my life as a "good gay Christian". I was easily deluded into thinking that when I died as long as I had been a "good person," the Lord would just look the other way concerning this "minor" flaw in my moral character.

I really believed, when I was a lukewarm Christian, that being the *"God loved everyone whether we obey His commandments or not"*- type Christian would be enough to get me into heaven. I thought I would have received a "basement condominium" in heaven and as far as I was concerned, as long as I got in, that would be fine.

Then when I started reading about what the Bible really has to say about homosexuality and sexual purity, my eyes began to open. Holy Scripture is very clear in its admonition that we are to be "holy temples" and "spotless brides" that are set apart.

The Lord restored my purity when He forgave me for all the years of sexual immorality that I had participated in, and even initiated. But soon after He washed away all the years of sexual sin. He then very gently pulled back the "velvet drape" of my life so that I could look at all the other sins that He wanted me to work on such as lying, greed, impatience, pride, etc.

Then the Lord began to show me that our walk with Him included a lifetime of commitment towards the challenge to "be holy because He is holy." The Church calls this sanctification. That's why the bumper sticker slogan put out by Alcoholics Anonymous is so powerful when it invites us to take <u>One Day at a Time</u>. We are constantly being made into His image.

Proverbs 27:5 tells us that the righteous man falls down seven times, but gets up seven times. The Lord's yoke is easy. He will never give us more than we can take. If God doesn't want you to be homosexual, he **will** give you the way out. You must trust that He is a loving God and wants to see you succeed, not fail.

Many of us raised in a home where our earthly father did not reflect the personality of the heavenly Father often have a skewed vision of just how loving God really is. If you were raised with a harsh father, you will think of God as harsh. If you were raised in a home where your father was absent either physically or psychologically, you may not be able to think that there is a dependable God out there. But I am here to say that if you seek the Lord with your whole heart and soul, He will reveal Himself to you. It is His desire to woo the children of Abraham (the true spiritual Israel) to His side. And His purpose *will* be done.

You must never give up! That's the main mission of Satan—having people renounce their faith in Jesus. Just remember: whenever they burned some of the Church's greatest saints at the stakes, the "saint in making" was always tempted by his/her accusers with the statement, *"Renounce your faith in Jesus, and you will not burn."* St. Joan of Arc prayed for her tormentors as she burned at the stake. And more important Jesus, in His great love for His enemies, cried out as He died, "Forgive them Father, for they know not what they do." Remember, if you don't give up on God, He will **never** give up on you.

We must also remember that not everyone in the gay political movement is evil. Many are naïve and don't realize that they are being used as pawns of the devil; however, many in this movement are out to destroy the traditional Judeo-Christian fiber that made America great.

Witchcraft and the New Age are the religions of many in high places within the gay political movement. It is a spirit of Antichrist that must be resisted at all costs. Their movement is inextricably tied to the abortion and feminist agendas. Many women and men who have been victims of sexual and other abuse in their childhood are easy prey to the gay political movement. The feminist women's colleges in America are now training grounds for the gay movement. Their mottos are, "You're not a woman until you've slept with one." They are being taught that men are no longer necessary and naïve parents all over this country are sending their children to these horrible schools.

This powerful gay agenda has now infiltrated the American Psychiatric Association (APA) and the other professional psychiatric associations, the National Education Association (NEA) and other professional education associations. Most of the major universities have bought into this PC message, and now the activists are coming after our children all the way down into the local elementary schools.

The gay activists have formed a new group called the Gay Lesbian Straight Teachers Education Network

(GLSTEN) whose mission is the homosexualization of our children. They know that most Americans over 45 are too smart to accept the tenets of this horrible agenda; so, they are going after our youth, not necessarily to make them gay but to **neutralize** them into accepting the gay agenda. **The gays don't have to get you completely into their camp, they have only to confuse you and/or neutralize you, and they've won**.

Consensus in the United States at the time this book was written is that 48% of the population supports the great majority of the gay agenda. This is frightening. Parents must teach their children to be compassionate to homosexuals; however they must be taught never to accept their agenda. If the younger generation doesn't stand strong on the issues of morality, this country is finished. Sexually promiscuity played a major role in the demise of both the Ancient Greek and Roman Empires.

The situation is grim and is getting grimmer. If a revival doesn't soon come in this country, beginning with the Church of Jesus Christ, I believe the Lord will pass judgment on the United States. Someone mentioned to me once that the United States isn't even mentioned as a power in the last day accounts in the book of Revelation. I am becoming more and more convinced that either the U.S. will cease to exist before the very end or that it may end up becoming the great whore of Babylon that is mentioned in Revelation 14.

We have bragged to the rest of the world for almost 250 years that we are one nation that serves the God of Abraham, Isaac and Jacob. We have even had the audacity to call this country Christian. Is this still true in the year 2009, or are we a **post Judeo-Christian country** that might contain some remnant Christians?

Have we allowed many different gods and goddesses into this country and then sent out all of our ambassadors to the farthest parts of the world peddling our "cup of abomination?" I pray not! **What most persons in this country don't fully realize is this: When the gay political agenda succeeds, the rest of America will fail. Now is the time to take action.**

If the next presidential election doesn't produce a leader who has a healthy fear of God, if the next president doesn't work diligently in his next administration to undo the anti-Christian campaign that has been mounting against America, if he doesn't move towards overturning Roe vs. Wade, and if he doesn't slap this very spoiled child called the gay political movement on the bottom and say, "No more!," then I believe our country is doomed.

As many as three Supreme Court seats will need to be filled during the next 5 years. If the next president doesn't place morally sound Christians on the bench of our highest court of this land, we might as well look for a new country to raise our children in. The Reagan and George H. Bush administrations failed us when they nominated "moderates" to the bench and the Clinton administration further disappointed us with the nomination of Judge Ginsburg.

The next presidential administration will determine the path the United States will take. Will it be a path of light, or further darkness?

Whatever path the American voters choose will determine her fate, however the Christian Church must continue to offer the hope of Jesus Christ no matter what the outcome of the next election produces. So, my fellow American Christians, will you join me in this valiant holy battle? Will you help spread the gospel to the homosexual struggler who yearns to be free? Will you continue to defend the spiritual orphans in our midst? Welcome aboard, because the harvest is ripe and the sowers are few!

I have felt the release of the Holy Spirit to preach the "Good News" as a born-again believer filled with the fire of Pentecost, having a great desire for the Lord to use the awesome story that He has put in my mouth that glorifies the never-ending power of the cross to redeem. The great majority of the wounds of my childhood and early adult life have healed; however, the scars are still there as a constant reminder of where I have come from... and to remind me to remain humble for He has done great things for me. Holy is His name!

Only through His Son's shed blood could such a testimony be manifested. Although I believe that my testimony will be used as an encouragement for people who have a desire to leave their homosexuality at the Cross so they may be reconciled to God, I am now further convinced that He will also use it to reconcile a body of believers back to its head, Jesus Christ. May God Bless You abundantly!

REFERRAL NETWORK AND RECOMMENDED BOOK LIST

Approved Suggested Reading List

There are now over 100 books on healing from homo-sexuality, sexual addiction and co-dependency. The majority are Christ-centered and can be found at the Homo-sexuals Anonymous website **ha-fs.org** or the Exodus website **exodusbooks.org.** You will also find a complete synopsis of each book on the two websites. I have listed my favorites below. Please look at both book websites. I can't recommend every book on both sites, however. I strongly disagree with some of the content of the books that are not on my approved list so be careful what you order. AAF.

1. Homosexuality: A New Christian Ethic, Dr. Elizabeth Moberly
2. Homosexuality and the Politics of Truth, Dr. Jeff Satinover
3. Healing the Masculine Soul, LeAnne Payne
4. The Life Recovery Bible, Tyndale Press
5. You Don't Have to Be Gay, Jeff Konrad
6. Lord Set Me Free (14 Step Recovery Workbook), H. A. website

7. Questions I Am Most Asked About Homosexuality, Sy Rogers
8. Crisis in Masculinity, LeAnne Payne
9. Women Who Love Sex Addicts, Doug Weiss & DianneDeBusk
10. The Bondage Breaker, Dr. Neil Anderson
11. The Heart of Female Same-sex Attraction, Janelle Hallman
12. A Way of Escape, Dr. Neil Anderson
13. Sexual Healing Workbook, Rev. David Kyle Foster
14. Door of Hope for the Sexually Abused, (6 CD set) Jan Frank & DK Foster
15. Healing for Damaged Emotions, David Seamands
16. Every Man's Battle (porno addiction), Steve Arterburn
17. Emotional Dependency, (great booklet) Lori Rentzel
18. Telling the Truth to Troubled People, William Backus
19. Pursuing Sexual Wholeness, Andy Comiskey
20. One of the Boys, (great Audio CD) Sy Rogers
21. Can Homosexuality be Healed?, Francis MacNutt

Parents & Friends Ministries
1551 N Flagler Dr.
West Palm Beach, Florida 33401
(561) 655-3055
parentsandfriends.com
Office Hours: Mon.-Fri. 9:30AM-5:30PM EST

Parents & Friends Ministries is a Christ-centered ministry offering hope to homosexual strugglers and their families. This organization believes that homosexuals are not born that way and can be healed and move towards a healthy heterosexual lifestyle. Resources: Annual National Ex-gay Conference offered in the spring. free information,

St Augustine's Sexual Healing Bookstore, website, phone counseling, speaking engagements, Church seminars.

Courage
210 W 31st Street
New York, New York 10001
(212) 268-1010
Rev. John Harvey/ National Director

Courage is a Roman Catholic Ministry offering support to persons experiencing same sex attractions who desire to live chaste lives in accordance with the teachings of the Catholic Church. Resources Available:100 spiritual support groups, EnCourage(for parents, spouse, family and friends support group), free information, speaking engagements, seminars and an annual national conference.

Homosexual Anonymous
P.O. Box 7881
Reading, PA 19603
(610) 376-1146

Homosexuals Anonymous (H.A.) is a non-denomi-national Christian organization offering Christ centered support for those that struggle with homosexual attractions. Resources Available: Over fifty-five chapters mainly located in the United States. Format of meetings are very close to the Alcoholics Anonymous (A.A.) Program but H.A. has returned to the biblical principles that allowed A.A. to prosper in the early 1930's. Wonderful 14–step self-help workbook, on-line chapters, newsletter, extensive book-ministry list, seminars, correspondence ministry and annual conference.

Pastoral Care Ministries
P.O. Box 1313
Wheaton, IL 60189
LeAnne Payne-Director

An international ministry focusing on inner healing (healing the hurts and scars of your childhood). Six annual conferences, in different parts of the United States providing deep inner healing for the sexually broken and victims of generational sin. In my opinion one of the best Christ-centered conferences offered in the U.S. dealing with the underlying issues that fuel a homosexual disorientation.

INDEX

Advocate (*Gay Newspaper*), 48
Allen, Starla, 82
American Psychiatric Association (*APA*), 116, 161, 221

Bloomfield, NJ, 16
Boo, Kate, 117, 122, 172
Boston, MA, 54-7, 61-3, 69, 70, 74, 158, 213
Brown, Bob (*Metanoia Ex-gay Ministry*) 101, 185
Bruno (*Porn Star*) 189-90
Bush Administration, 126, 233

Carnegie Institute (The), 150-1
Cathedral of the Sacred Heart of Jesus, (Newark, NJ), 59, 66,
Catholic Archdiocese of Washington, DC, 123, 125
Christopher Street, New York, 33, 36
Clinton, President Bill and Hillary, 172-3, 223
Cohn, Roy, 34, 36, 38, 40-2, 44

Dobson, Dr. James / Focus on the Family, 168-71

Ever-Straight Encourager, 207-8
Episcopal Church, 111

CPSIA information can be obtained at www.ICGtesting.com
Printed in the USA
BVOW07s0926291014

372784BV00001B/212/P